I0346283

OPEN YOUR HEART TO THE TRUE YOU:

A Useful Handbook to Finding Happiness

Renee Salvatori

PUBLISHING
Green Bay, WI 54311

Open Your Heart To the True You: A Useful Handbook to Finding Happiness by Renee Salvatori, copyright © 2015, 2017 by Renee Salvatori. This title was originally published as *May Your Heart Be Light* © 2013 by Renee Salvatori. All rights reserved.
Reflexology of the Feet Chart © 2013 by Stacy Simone.
Preface by Mary Roberts © 2017 by Mary Roberts.

Thank you to the following for allowing Renee Salvatori to reprint your beautiful quotations.
Quotation by Philip Simmons. Permission to reprint by Kathryn Field.
Quotation by Stephen C. Paul. Permission to reprint by Stephen C. Paul.
Quotations by Ram Dass. Permission to reprint by Ram Dass.
Quotation by Robert Fulghum. Permission to reprint by Robert Fulghum.
Quotation by the Dalai Lama. Permission to reprint by His Holiness the Dalai Lama.
Quotation by Sakyong Mipham Rinpche. Permission to reprint by Sakyong Mipham.
Quotation by Alan Cohen. Permission to reprint by Alan Cohen.
Quotation by Dr. Edgar Mitchell. Permission to reprint by Dr. Mitchell.

This book is designed to provide information and motivation to our readers. It is sold with the understanding that the publisher is not engaged to render any type of medical, psychological, legal, or other professional advice. The content herein is the sole expression and opinion of the author. This book is not meant to be used, nor should it be used, to diagnose or treat any medical condition. For diagnosis or treatment of any medical problem, consult your own physician. Neither the author nor the publisher shall be liable for any physical, psychological, emotional, financial, or commercial damages, including, but not limited to, special, incidental, consequential, or other damages. References are provided for informational purposes only and do not constitute endorsement of any websites or other sources. Readers should be aware that the websites listed in this book may change. Our views and rights are the same: You are responsible for your own choices, actions, and results.

This book is based on the real life experiences of Renee Salvatori of Wheeling, West Virginia. This book reflects the opinions of the author and her life's decisions. Written Dreams Publishing does not approve, condone or disapprove of these opinions. It is up to the reader to make their own decisions.

All rights reserved. In accordance with the U.S. Copyright Act of 1976, no part of this publication may be reproduced, distributed, or transmitted in any form or by any means, or stored in a database or retrieval system, without prior written permission of the publisher, Written Dreams Publishing, Green Bay, Wisconsin 54311. To contact the publisher, visit writtendreams.com.

This book is licensed for your personal enjoyment only. This book may not be re-sold or given away to other people. If you would like to share this book with another person, please purchase an additional copy for each recipient. If you're reading this book and did not purchase it, or it was not purchased for your use only, then please purchase your own copy. Thank you for respecting the hard work of this author.

Editing: Brittiany Koren and Susan Pawlicki
Cover art design and layout: Ed Vincent/ENC Graphics
Artwork: Logan Stefonek
Category: Self-Help/Motivational
Description: *Renee Salvatori chronicles her journey on how she found happiness with herself and the world.*
Library of Congress Catalog number: Applied for.
Hard Cover ISBN: 978-0-9987623-0-2
Paperback ISBN: 978-0-9981673-8-1
Ebook ISBN: 978-0-9987623-1-9

Revised Edition published by Written Dreams Publishing, March 2017.

Contents

Preface	7
Introduction	9
Going Within	10
Enlightenment	15
Research, Research, Research	20
Mirror Help	22
Be Kind to Yourself	26
Affirmations	32
Breathing	35
Worthiness	38
Relationships	42
Have an Opinion of Your Own	46
Individuated	49
Control and Judgment	52
Ego	57
Belief Systems	59
Emotion	65
Prayer	68
Meditation	71
God or Creator	79
Religion and Church	83
Angels	87
Anger and Release	94
Death and Reincarnation	100
Soul and Spirit	108
Karma	111
Negatives into Joy	119
Energy Medicine	127

Contents

Chakra 134
Simplify 145
Busy Overload 149
Essences from Nature 155
Find a Creative Outlet 158
Health and Other Snippets 161
Astrology 173
Closing 178
Ending Quote 182
Excerpt from Open Your Mind to the True You ... 183
Glossary 191
Resources 195
Acknowledgements 198
About the Authors 200

Preface

Mary Roberts

When I first began to read *Open Your Heart to the True You* by Renee Salvatori, I had never met the woman. However, by the time I was halfway through the book, I felt like Renee and I'd been close friends for quite a while. Or maybe I was getting to know myself a little better with the help of her stories. My deepest gratitude for her bravery, and sharing her inspiration with us. It took a lot of courage!

In our world today of unending compromise, life can deliver some daunting surprises. Often throughout a lifetime we are challenged to look for a safe place where we can recover from life crises or traumas—a place to release pain and promote the healing processes to find ourselves again. Renee's research and lifetime work offers that safe harbor and gives the reader ideas for the best places to start this process. Keeping an open heart and mind after the metamorphosis can help us discover who we really are, and our true potentials. To begin, it's worth the process of relief to look at who we really are now. In the big picture, this effort will ultimately improve your health and open up your mind to the true you you're longing to become.

I can't begin to express how much it's worth taking the self-challenge to restore your heart, your mind, and your soul. Reach for your goals and challenge yourself for *you*, and a better world.

Renee shows us a starting place of incredible resources in which to begin your new journey. Use them wisely and reflect often. "Remember, all the world is a stage." When you dance, please be kind and gentle with the people that you love.

Introduction

Writing this book has felt so very right to me. It has fulfilled me in a way I cannot explain. Herein are my truths and experiences. My writings are a product of these experiences that shape who I am. As you read my experiences, you may find many similarities from your school of life. You are all in here somewhere, either loudly in the words or quietly between the lines.

I write of my truths today as I understand them today. I talk with you not as an expert, but as a continual seeker. I am a lover of much that I want to share, and I hope you will feel casualness as you read this. I wish these pages to be casual, as if we were sitting across from one another, friend to friend, having a chat. There is no order to the chapters, so you can pick which topic you would like to go to first. There is nothing you have to do. There is nothing you have to feel. Just enjoy your moments of reflection. Let the words go through you and stay if you feel they are of benefit to you.

I have also shared wonderful quotes that have touched my life and pulled me along. One of my favorites is by James Oppenheim, "The foolish man seeks happiness in the distance, but the wise grow it under his feet." If you are searching for that little extra something in your life, I urge you to start today, somehow and some way right where you stand, right where you are reflecting. Our betterment and contentment should never be put off. Waiting takes it into the future (tomorrow, next week, or next year). The future is never really here because it is always out there somewhere. This betterment or contentment needs to come in the "now." Today is just waiting for you to join in.

My hope is that this book helps you find some peace, health, and happiness. Anything you glean from my book or any other searches should have an ease to it. If it doesn't flow nicely for you, then struggling with it will only bring pain and frustration. May the reflections of your own heart and mind lead you with gentle ease into a better space. May your heart be light, just as my heart has been made light again in sharing with you.

*"What within me needs to die?
Out of this death what resurrection
will come?"*
—Philip Simmons from *Learning to Fall*

Going Within

Whether we know it or not, we are all on a path of alignment every single day. When we crawl out of bed and place our feet on the floor, we instinctually align our posture to hold our full weight into a standing position. This act is like breathing, and we do not think about it. Internal alignment is also instinctual, and we do not necessarily need to think about it, but sometimes we have to give thoughtful attention to things that are usually instinctual. Perhaps we hurt our back or just felt weak. In those cases, we'd need to give attention to how we place our feet and our body weight before standing. Our internal alignment can also demand thoughtful attention. We may feel a little off-center and need to focus on finding balance. Finding our balance, alignment, or enlightenment is our birthright. Some people blend into this part of life easily; others go kicking and screaming. I was a kicker and a screamer. I didn't have cancer or a major illness propelling me into my many searches, but it was an illness just the same. It was the disease of relentless DIS-EASE, or the complete opposite of ease. I was being pulled into a riptide and was sinking into frustration and anxiety. I was pulled further and further under, and little unexplained sicknesses started popping up. I didn't even know where to begin to start healing myself. I needed help.

My upbringing was built on what I now feel was fanatical control, based on religion and fear. We were never encouraged to think for ourselves, and all teachings were propelled through this fear of never being perfect enough.

Even though I gave the religion up shortly after I got married, the seeds of conflict had been born. When I became interested in healing myself, I had all kinds of questions. Where could I start? What practices were safe? A friend of mine who was fighting cancer asked me to go with her to a series of group therapy sessions followed by meditation. I hesitated at first, but I felt she needed my support, so I agreed to go. Little did I know I was the one to be supported in the very early stages of my searching!

After the opening session of talk, we ended with a meditation of soft, peaceful music. I closed my eyes as everyone else did, but one eye popped open continually to see what everyone else was doing. I had never seen or participated in a meditation. I didn't know what to think, but I slowly began to relax into it. At a young age I was taught meditation was bad, but now I wondered, why? I felt relaxed and connected, and my fear was replaced with tranquility. I went home and started reading about meditation, not from my more judgmental church resources, but from non-biased resources. I also started to listen to CDs on meditating. This started me on a journey, and I was compelled to keep going. I didn't quite understand just then, but I was being liberated.

I think there is nothing more frustrating than trying to prepare for something without knowing what you're preparing for. With holidays, for example, you prepare because you know what is coming. With this feeling I had, I wasn't sure what exactly I was preparing for or even how to prepare. I felt like I was spinning my wheels. I had one foot on the gas pedal and one foot on the brake AT THE SAME TIME. I was very busy parenting, but I still felt empty and hollow, purposeless. I asked myself, "Why am I here?" I'd spent years visiting churches without finding what I needed. I gave up looking for a church and gravitated to other things. What I did understand from all those searches outside of myself was I needed to start inside myself first. My yearning to prepare for myself continued, and I also continued to look for the truer and better me. The more I stopped fighting the process and went inward on my journey, the more clarity I found. I no longer had one foot on the gas and one foot on the brake. I was moving forward into my journey of self. The journey was slow, but it was steady.

I also realized, through my experiences in the school of life, that I had learned many things and I could now take what felt right for me. Did a teaching resonate with me? Did it feel like my truth? What I realized was there are many truths, either written or verbal, which are not my truths or truths that felt right for me. There is no one "truth," just as there is no one personality. There are as many truths as there are people. Even if we are all fed the same food or information, each of us will digest it differently. Remember sitting in class and how some students seemed to relate to what the teacher said and some didn't? The students' ability to relate to the teacher wasn't objectively good or bad; it was just different. We are all different, and this world holds so much diversity to enjoy. I can like spring while you may like summer. If a thought or idea feels good to you, then it is your truth. Everyone's journeying will be different and diverse. Free will is truly a gift; do not give it away by ignoring it or accepting others' truths as yours. Take your gift and your truths, and enjoy them. There is so much liberation in knowing your own truths!

If you are doing something in your life that isn't working, doing more of it will not make it work any better. Nothing can be resolved if you keep trying to fix unworkable situations with the same consciousness that created them. You will need to search for a different approach, a different way, or a different truth. If your life seems sick, stressful, unexciting, or limited, this is an indication something is missing. Have you allowed yourself to stop growing? Let your true inner soul connect to your physical self.

I needed a lot of "reprogramming" and purging of old ways of thinking and being so my newly evolved self could be built. Some of my outdated ideas had to die so newness could be birthed, and some outgrown ways needed to casually fall away like a forgotten but beloved toy. Do you refuse to grow by holding onto old ways and beliefs because they feel comfortable? If a snake refused to shed its skin for its growing body, it would get sick and die because its body would be so compressed and compacted. A snake shedding its skin is a natural process. Can you find natural ways to grow into your new self?

We all have to make our own changes. No one is going to change for us; that would be like one snake telling another snake he had to shed his skin. If the skin isn't ready for shedding, the uncovered skin is raw and unusable. If that same know-it-all snake told the other snake to shed far too late, then disease and bacteria would be attached to the shriveled up skin. Change, and when it happens, is our choosing and our journey. It is our own evolution and our own rhythm.

Love yourself enough to nurture yourself today and tomorrow, and you will find that you aren't abandoning yourself anymore. Gautama Buddha once said, "You can look the whole world over and never find anyone more deserving of love then yourself." If we want changes in our lives, we have to love our souls and patiently nurture them through the healing process. We all proceed and move forward with our own abilities and strengths. Some of us will advance with courage, some with patience, and some with purpose. All of us will find our own reasons and our own techniques.

If you are holding this book in your hands, your soul is probably searching. I hope each day propels you further into your searches. I hope you find the healing and betterment you desire. It is yours for the taking; claim it! Believe in yourself and your ability to get what you desire. Love yourself enough to try. As you take each step along the way, you will start to see your enlightenment. If you read this book with the thought that you need to be fixed, your mind will be focused only on what is wrong with you. There is nothing wrong with you. There is everything right with you! You are capable of taking care of yourself, so pat yourself on the back for the gifts and the talents you already embrace. You are probably further along than you realize. As you turn within, you may find more answers waiting. Appreciate all the things about yourself as you proceed in this book and in your life.

Never abandon the physical part of yourself for the spiritual part of yourself. We are born into our physical bodies for a reason. We were born to see, touch, taste, hear, and smell. We are not meant to live only a spiritual life or only a physical life. Our whole being, both spiritual and physical, should be of equal importance to us and well blended together. We can relate this to food and water. We would not deliberately dehydrate or starve ourselves in order to only drink or only eat. When we are thirsty, we drink. When we are hungry, we eat. We see the value of food and water blending. If either the food or the water balance is neglected, we take longer to get back into a healthy state. Give your whole body the optimal gift now and maintain both the spiritual and the physical. It is easier to maintain balance than to try to recover after you are severely out of balance.

Do not resist an opportunity for growth. After all those years of taking mental notes on how you envisioned yourself to be, now is the time to bloom! We don't have to hold onto the past anymore; we can grow into the beautiful flower we've seen ourselves as being.

See your goal, reach that goal, and then reach for another, continuing to pull from all your strengths and wisdoms.

There will come a time when we stop expecting others to give us the answers to life or matters of the heart, and we start finding them ourselves. Yes, finding answers can be hard and frustrating. I much preferred others' answers to my dilemmas because I was used to being spoon-fed and told what to think, believe, and feel for so long. It felt unnatural going solo and thinking for myself. It unnerved me and made me feel uncomfortable. I was used to receiving others' thoughts, opinions, and directions, and I assumed theirs was the right way, even when it wasn't. I gave others more credit than I gave myself. I found, though, when I took off and flew that even if I got an answer wrong, I could switch course and try something else. "Wrong" is only an indication of a way that didn't work. Nothing is ever set in stone. Your thoughts and truths will change.

Now comes the time for patience as you weave your own tapestry. Patiently search out your own answers, going within to see if the answers are for you. Before you know it, your self-alignment will be as instinctual as breathing and standing. What you need will come naturally, and you will just know. Enjoy your journeying into true knowingness and liberation!

"If you have built castles in the air, your work need not be lost; that is where they should be. Now put foundations under them."
—Henry David Thoreau

Enlightenment

So just what is enlightenment? It is that alignment you find from going within, the fullness of you that reveals your clarity, stability, sureness, and certainty. Enlightenment is letting go of what holds you down or bothers you. It is finding ways of making everything lighter in your life. Enlightenment is also being in that light of self and standing in your power. It is forward movement or evolution, the awakening and development of the inner self or the true, authentic you. It is you that lives deep within and radiates outward. Enlightenment is finding your own inner guidance and striving toward your full potential. As you can see, enlightenment can mean so much. Which of these thoughts means enlightenment to you?

The dictionary defines *enlightenment* as, "A final blessed state marked by the absence of desire or suffering. It is freedom from ignorance and misinformation." That's a powerful description. Wouldn't the absence of internal and external suffering be welcomed?

We all long for inner peace, tranquility, and calm. We can all have it by making daily efforts to change how we view ourselves, others, and the world. Sometimes enlightenment comes through the difficult times, when we are brought to our knees in order to make a change. It was in those moments, on my knees, that I both vowed to make a change and was most open to accept that change. Patience and nurturing will be needed as you grow, just like children need to be nurtured with sleep, nutrition, and love so their bodies can grow and develop. Find ways to nurture yourself as you expand into your new enlightenment.

Growing can sometimes be challenging. It can be like the physical growing you experienced as a child. Sometimes the measurements on the wall indicated a major growth spurt. That growth spurt may have come with growing pains. Your mother may have rubbed your legs to ease the pain, or you may have soaked in the tub. This growth hurt, but it had to happen. Do you also remember the emotional growing that accompanied puberty? Your emotions grew and proved challenging too, but you didn't try to stop the growth, even though it was complex. Sometimes as we are walking through the storm of growth, we beg it to go away, but we have to keep going through the thunder and lightning to reach the other side and sunshine.

Spiritual growth can also be difficult because we can feel abandoned in our darkest hours. This darkness or growth can be compared to the protective womb of a mother. There was no light in our mothers' wombs, yet we grew wonderfully there. We needed that dark space to prepare for our birth, and when we emerged, we were prepared for the world. Sometimes our darkness is preparing us for our enlightenment or new birth. We can also compare this process to the earth's days and nights. If all we had were sun-filled days, then the earth would become overheated. The night comes in to sooth and refresh. Sometimes our own darkness is for our protection, refreshment, and growth. Light and dark will balance themselves out, so be patient.

Our parents and our past can be true indicators of our emotions. They can be our gauges to see how we have changed, grown, and expanded. When we spend time with our parents, family members, or friends, we may be confronted with old ways and patterns. We may, unknowingly, resort to those old patterns of thinking we have worked so hard to leave behind. Rahm Dass said, "If you think you are so enlightened, spend a week with your parents." Isn't that a wonderful test? When you doubt that you have ever expanded, revisit the past. If you ever feel challenged or struggling while visiting those old ways from a human, a memory, or a movie, use this technique that has helped me many times. Go to a sink and run your hands under cool water. The cool water can also be splashed on your face with great benefit. This will bring you back to the "new and improved you" while the water washes the old patterns back down the drain.

There are many possibilities for nurturing ourselves as we go forward.

Stay open to people or learning possibilities. Do not hold thoughts of how you think you should be helped. This only limits the support that can come, and you may miss some great benefits. When we relax, we are able to see more options. Teachers are everywhere and plentiful. Some teach by good example, and some teach us by what not to do. We could learn from an old wise person or a young innocent child. A teacher may be a physical being, a book that practically jumps off a shelf to be read, a friend, or even the "teacher" emerging within you. Has this already started for you? All advancement is generated by your willingness. It has to be generated by you! Remember, teachers may open the door, but you walk in yourself.

My earliest example of this came when I started praying and asking for help with my son, as traditional medicine wasn't working for him. I heard about a naturopathic doctor in a big city an hour away but did not know her name. When I finally found her, I asked her why she didn't advertise so people could find her. She said she felt that those sincerely seeking her way of healing would find her when they were ready. She explained that people couldn't be coerced into her program unless they were willing. I didn't understand at first. The point was brought home for me years later when we were experiencing good results with this doctor. I tried to convince some of my extended family members to use her products. I purchased some items for them to try, only to find those items years later unopened and expired. In my excitement, I had forced my findings on them. It didn't work, nor should it have. Just as in our own search for spiritual enlightenment, we should not force others into our ways, no matter how well intentioned. We can share little tidbits of what we are learning if others are interested, but sharing is not recruiting. We all find our own teachers and light bearers when we are ready.

We need to honor that each of us is in a different grade or stage of growth. We are not the same spiritual age. Older in years may not be better. We are not all working with the same knowledge, insights, experiences, or connection to our own souls. How could a person who has never experienced cancer truly understand the life of a cancer patient? How could an unmarried person understand a married couple? Life has too many variables. There are too many differences in each of us to allow us to travel down someone else's road. Everyone is doing the best he can, using what he currently has to work with. So, no judgment or guilt directed to self or others. We only need to focus on our own needs and then commit to taking care of those.

Have faith and trust that all will flow to you at the right time. In the movie *Field of Dreams*, Kevin Costner was building a baseball field out of blind faith because he kept hearing the words, "Build it and they will come." He did things in the preparation but did not know who, if anyone, would come. When we start to build to our own enlightened path, the encouragement, teachers, and help will come. Just keep building and moving forward, even if it feels like blind faith. It is also like the little saying, "Leap and the net will appear."

You do not have to accept all you hear, see, and read. Like a buffet table with many food choices, you get to choose your preferences. All will choose different portion sizes and will describe the tastes differently. That buffet table may be set up with dishes of prayer, meditation, reading, exercise, Reiki, body healing, motivational tapes, etc. Your plate may hold a large portion of meditation and a small portion of prayer. The person next to you may have a large portion of prayer, a small portion of meditation, with only a condiment of Reiki. You will find that which is right for you. There is no race. Slow but steady always wins the race. Isn't that the story of "The Tortoise and the Hare"? Go slow and steady on your new path.

I do want to mention that when we commit to our new path, sometimes our relationships can also change. If you have a friendship/relationship that began when you were focused on a certain way of living, you may feel yourself pulling away from that relationship as you focus on other ways. Your interests may grow apart. The law of attraction says we are attracted to people who are on the same wave length. Someone focused on love and peace won't be attracted to people who focus on fear and negativity. Every relationship serves a purpose, even the short-lived ones. Sometimes, when a purpose has been served, the attraction between two people or a person and a group may end. Ask Divine Guidance for healings, peace, and direction for you and all involved through these shifts or endings.

Just when you think you are sailing along, you might face a setback. This is okay because we are still living, which means we have many things going on. These setbacks could be fear, sickness of self or loved ones, or financial issues, for example, and our inner guidance and faith can be challenged. If we never have setbacks, we have never changed or we are in a dead state. Think of how boring that would be!

Helen Keller said, "The great thing in the world is not so much where we stand as in what direction we are moving." Stay present and keep moving forward to your truths. There is a saying, "Man, I keep moving one step forward and two steps back." Well, that's okay because in the final round, you are still moving forward, even if it is slowly. Remember, as we said, slow and steady wins the race. There may also come a time when you think that you have learned all there is to know or you have reached the peak of everything you want to be. That will only be the beginning. We always get another chance since we're never finished. Isn't that a redeeming thought? Find your enlightenment in your alignment of all you long to be in trueness to yourself. There are so many opportunities to continue forward to renewed strength and growth. Many wonderful journeys and searches lie ahead!

"Knowledge is power."
—Sir Francis Bacon

Research, Research, Research

It is natural to want to learn and grow. It is also advantageous and healthy to expand into your discoveries. Henry David Thoreau encouraged us to "live deep and suck all the marrow of life." It does not matter your age or abilities. We all have a deep longing to be all that we can be. Continue to feed your hungry longings. The world belongs to the endlessly curious. It belongs to those who experience the world with eyes wide open and to those who never stop exploring, discovering, and evolving. We explore through travel, reading, contemplating, doing, walking in nature, and just watching the world breathe around us. The possibilities the world holds for us are endless. Not only can you explore the external world by reading a book, but you can also explore the interior world of you.

Don't feel overwhelmed with all the learning methods available. Try asking Divine Power or the angels to point you in a learning direction. Reading motivational articles or books and listening to good motivational DVDs and CDs are good places to start. I surrounded myself with things like meditation, chakra learning, body energy, positive movies and reading, peaceful music, motivational speakers, anger releasing techniques, and so many other ideas that, as I sought knowledge, would just pop out and ask me to take them home. They all became my friends for a while. I got a portable CD player. These little players can go anywhere. They can be used while your partner or room buddy is sleeping. This let me learn on the go and at my convenience while not disturbing others. It allowed me to designate my listening time. My family could watch TV while I listened with my headphones to my own choice of inspiration. Where there's a will, there's a way, and many of these ways are free! Libraries have books, CDs, and DVDs available. If your local library is a lending library, it can call around to other libraries to see if they have the book, CD, DVD, or magazine article you are searching for at the moment. Use their lending system. For me, this research of reading and listening was not just for entertainment but also for my enlightenment. I began to be awakened to my positive potentials.

After you have gotten filled up with your new discoveries, you will want to put them into practice. You will have confidence and will not need all the encouragement you needed in the beginning. Yes, you will continue to need encouragement, but it is in the beginning that you need it the most. Once you are propelled, the momentum will be there. Those learned discoveries will flow from memory, and you can use what you need at appropriate times. Those memory whispers will be your greatest advisors and security as you now integrate them into your full self. Aristotle said, "Educating the mind without educating the heart is no education at all." Learn all you need and feel from the deepest reserves of your soul. So, go ahead and "live deep and suck all the marrow out of life." In your today and tomorrows, may you continue to explore.

> *"Mirror, mirror on the wall, who's the fairest of them all?"*
> —Brothers Grimm, 1812 fairy tale

Mirror Help

Mirror therapy, as I call it, was so important to me. It was the one step that truly helped me find myself and was where I experienced my biggest growth. It was the springboard that helped me jump into other important things. Sounds like the easiest task, but it *was one of the hardest things I have ever done*. In those moments of work, I cried my deepest cries. So don't be fooled by how simple it sounds. The main idea is *you* talking to *"you"* in the mirror. You can let your guard down and be honest as you do this because you are the only one to see or hear it.

Begin by looking at yourself in the mirror and smile. Sounds easy so far, ay? What did you get back after you looked at yourself? Did you find that you quickly looked away or that you stared at yourself, analyzing your perceived flaws? Did you get a smile or resistance? *Keep looking no matter what you see*, and as you begin to look deep into your eyes, allow you to love what you see, no matter what your ego tells you. Tell yourself, "I love you." Say this over and over, no matter how silly you think you sound. I began my "I love you's" haphazardly. I thought the idea was goofy, but what did I have to lose? I was at a low point and feeling unhappy. I said more "I love you's" and laughed, each time laughing harder. My laughing tears soon changed to crying tears. The floodgates opened, and I began to sob. It was an unexpected moment of truth that was so evident when I looked into my eyes. I didn't love myself. Oh, I could love others, but not myself? We are all here to love and be loved, but more importantly, we deserve the love of ourselves.

How amazing to give love to yourself and to receive it back from you. Think of that! Loving yourself can be one hard accomplishment!

How many of us base our underlying feelings of love on whether we feel loved by others? We all love that delicious feeling of being loved that truly swells the heart, but what if love from another is missing at a certain point in our lives? We can continue to feel that wonderful feeling by working and allowing our own self-love. Do we really need others to make us whole or to fill those dark voids? Try to work on the neglected area of love without relying on another for it. Again, it can be one difficult task, but don't give up.

This mirror work was truly a turning point for me. I began to take my ability to love myself seriously. I ate healthier foods. I gave myself needed sleep. I asked for downtime to nurture myself. I became a *self-ish* person. I became all of the self's: self-love, self-centered, self-controlled, self-starter, self-helped, and self-propelled. I began to associate positive emotions with all those "self" words I used to be so afraid of. They became my friends. They look selfish when viewed negatively, but really, they are not selfish when viewed in a healthy, positive way.

I had never given myself permission to do what I liked and needed to do. Now I began to give myself meditation time, journaling time, sleep-in time, reading, walking, or something as simple as nothingness time to analyze how I was doing. I began to focus on me. I asked myself, "What can I do for you today? What about a relaxing bath?" Wow, I hadn't done that in years. Is that selfish?

I gave myself time-out from simple responsibilities. I taught the kids, depending on their ages, to do more work: laundry, cleaning the toilets, and dusting their own rooms. This allowed me time for my own endeavors. I realized I had all along taught *them* it was okay to personally relax and chill out, but I never allowed myself the same luxury. I began to listen to music I wanted to hear. My children didn't have to control the car stereo knobs all the time. It sounds so simple, but it may not feel so simple if you have always allowed yourself to be last. Keep making time for yourself a priority. Once you start putting the SELF into yourself, please don't let guilt settle in. You stood up for yourself, now don't pull yourself back down with the ever-famous guilt factor. Shake it off as quickly as you can. Remind yourself, "I deserve and am willing to allow myself a brief uninterrupted connection to myself. All I am doing is pausing and not abandoning." And then repeat that as you enjoy your cup of coffee or that evening stroll without little followers. So many people say they can't make time for themselves, but the truth is you can't afford not to make time. More connected relationships begin with a connection to self first.

I hope you will give yourself the time you need to grow. We all need a half-hour to an hour a day (at least) for ourselves. How do you spend your time? Our teenagers come home and go to their rooms to "veg out" or listen to music. The younger ones head outside to play when their souls call them to touch nature and de-stress. One time, the noise and smells in the house were bothering me. One child was listening to music, two were watching television, and one was polishing her nails. I grabbed a blanket and told everyone I would be out in the backyard sitting in the grass. It wasn't long before two other bodies joined me. I actually asked them to go back inside and told them they could come out in thirty minutes. Sometimes we have to get our breathing room any possible way and that desire for alone time can be strong; it will give you strength to send two cute little bodies back into the house. I love children's giggles, but I needed to breathe the fresh air without sharing it. I needed to hear the birds sing without their giggles breaking the rhythm of the winged symphony. Desire can help you come up with other creative ways for finding your own space. I have sat in a parked car in the garage and hid behind our fence so I couldn't be easily eyeballed by the little ones. Of course, my husband was handy for their care, but I didn't want the "mommy always does it" look. A couple of times, I drove to a parking lot or scenic area just to sit by myself. You, too, will find ways to create your own time. How do you get air, de-stress, and be true to yourself? If being "selfish" seems too drastic for you, then tell your family you just need a time-out in your room. Oh, what you can do in a time-out.

I have realized that many people in our society tend to ignore themselves instead of looking for themselves. They avoid this true acknowledgment of self out of fear. They spend time worrying or concerning themselves with other people or things so they do not have to focus on themselves. When they do have to think about themselves, they also have to face what may need to be corrected, and this can be painful and scary. Other people disconnect from themselves and don't see anything they want to change because disconnect doesn't allow them to see clearly. They cannot tell themselves the life story of who they are and what they want. Some people even make themselves feel superior to compensate for this inferior, unloved feeling and thus believe all is well in their fairy tale.

But when you look into your eyes in that mirror, you cannot deny you anymore. When you look deep into your eyes, the soul of you, you will begin to find yourself again. You will know what you need, and you will begin to find ways to give yourself what is needed. This is how to love you. May you be given the courage to love yourself over and over again! May you find the "self" in yourself!

"Encouragement does more than criticism."
—Renee Salvatori

Be Kind to Yourself

Someone told me once I had open enemies. I pondered this fiercely. Open would mean people I knew. Well, who doesn't have enemies? Even a perfect man like Jesus did. After years of reflecting on this, I truly realized what was meant. The open enemy was not a dark figure in the alley, so to speak; it was me. I was my own worst and destructive enemy. Who is your enemy; is it another or is it yourself? We may be victims of others, but we may also be victims of ourselves.

As noted in the last chapter, I was not kind to myself. I was much kinder to those around me. I put others first and left very little time or energy for myself. If you've ever flown on a plane, you've seen and heard the statement, "Put your own air mask on first." If a plane is having trouble and you are told to put your air masks on, what happens if you lean over and first help all your family members to put their masks on properly? They are okay, but you are rapidly dissolving into frantic mode as you reach for your mask and find all your fingers have turned to thumbs. Fear and stress have escalated, and you resemble a panicked blob. It's almost too late, or maybe it's already too late. Your noble deed of helping others has left you lacking in your own personal care, and considering worst case scenario, what good is a dead parent or caregiver to the family? In the real world, what good is an unconscious human being? To survive sanely, you have to put your mask on first by learning ways to be kind to yourself.

Are we ourselves living in this same abandonment and poverty? Can we change our living arrangements and make ourselves rich and fulfilled by beginning to love ourselves? Love is the best form of kindness we can give ourselves. We all need nurturing, and we also need space to be nurtured in. We need to find ways to cultivate ourselves, both mentally and physically.

When I was young and my mother saw me do something unkind, she would say in a sing-song way something like, "Be kind in all you say and do, as words and actions will follow through." There is deep truth in those words. Who of us would not like kindness given to us by anyone, even by ourselves? Have you ever thought of how you make war against yourself as an enemy? Do you criticize yourself by calling yourself stupid? You wouldn't call your loved ones stupid if they forgot something or did something wrong. No doubt you would pick them up with encouragement. So why get down on yourself? Give yourself the same love and healing you give others. When we criticize ourselves, it is hard to make changes. When we love ourselves, it is easier. Remember, "Words and actions follow through." It is only when we learn to love ourselves, without stipulations or exceptions, that real change can be made. We love ourselves regardless of what others say, what you yourself may say, what you did or didn't do, what you feel or don't feel, or where you are or aren't at any given point in time. It is unconditional love which is true, whole, and entire. It places no conditions on you or others. It is a love no matter what. So smile at yourself, love yourself, and forgive yourself in all things big and small. Unconditional love is the greatest kind of love, not only for others, but for you as well.

Do you smile at others? Probably! Do you smile at yourself? Probably not! As you walk past a mirror, do you pause to smile at yourself instead of just to critique your appearance? Even when we silently criticize or dislike our bodies, we pull in negativity and criticism. This can make us unhealthy. There is a Yugoslavian proverb that says, "Good thoughts are half of good health." For our own sanity and health, we need to think kindly of and to ourselves. It is a vibration which has a ripple effect. Love allows love, which in turn can allow health and more health. Someone once said that in order to get anything done in the world, their everyday religion was to love themselves first, and everything else would fall into line. So start to love yourself and each step to a new you, and more love will come your way. Loving yourself and others will become easier and easier.

We all know how sad it is to lie to others, but we rarely feel remorse when we lie to ourselves. If we all drank a dose of truth serum, we would be quite surprised at our findings. Being honest with yourself and what you need is so very beneficial to being the best you can be to yourself. Has anyone ever asked you if you are happy, but you did not answer honestly because you did not want to hurt his feelings? Have you ever felt taken advantage of because you were not honest with others around you? Many times we stuff our true honest feelings down and later resent the other party or even ourselves, and then we distance ourselves from our true feelings even further. It is dishonesty at the grandest level and dishonesty is not kind.

Many of us prepare our outer body for meeting or hanging out with others. We comb our hair, brush our teeth, apply makeup, wear deodorant or body scents, and put on clean clothes. Have you ever thought of how you prepare internally? Is your outward cover the only nice thing? When I was younger, I never thought about preparing internally for myself, my future husband, or my children. I was a sponge and learned all I could in knowledge of how to be a good mother and wife, but those chocolate chip cookies I learned how to bake became my breakfast, lunch, and dinner. The many late nights never crossed my mind as abuse that would eventually catch up to me. Those little push down true feelings exercises only gave way to resentment over many years. Pushing my body beyond its breaking point physically and mentally only led to pure exhaustion and constant sickness.

When one pushes, it unconsciously creates resistance which creates resentment. Like a rubber band, if you keep pulling it outside its normal circumference, it will break and will not adequately be able to do the job it was made to do; you then resent the lousy job the rubber band did. The same idea is with our own lives. If we pull, push, and resist our normal boundary lines, we will not be able to adequately do our job, and we may begin to resent our lives or abilities. When I pushed too hard, I found I had less patience and fatigue formed everywhere in my body. Some days it even hurt to peel a carrot or hold a book to read to my children. I realized my quick-fix caffeine only allowed me to push harder when I needed to do less. I began to find ways to stay within my own circumference of wellness.

Be kind to your body with sleep. Do you stay up late, night after night, with the intentions of eventually catching up on your sleep over the weekend? Sleep is extremely beneficial to repairing and growing new cells. In sleep, our minds can sort out and purge the chatter of the day, so we get a refreshing and calm start for the new and upcoming day. If you are plagued by lack of sleep because of other physical, mental, and emotional issues, seek help from a professional. Without sleep, our bodies and minds deteriorate. In war, one choice of torture is sleep deprivation. The first year of parenting a new infant can also be a form of sleep deprivation, which is challenging because of all the interrupted sleep. Sleep deprivation is mental and physical suffering, and you begin to lose your mental faculties and health if you become too deprived. Say "No!" to the late night movies, video games, books, or computer programs so your sleep patterns will improve, along with your mind and health. I'm not talking about saying no to a crying infant or a sick family member; I'm only talking about those activities we can all become "trapped" by late at night.

Can you actually sit down and enjoy the meal nourishing your body? Or do you want to get up and "do" something at the same time? Do you eat healthy foods to recharge your tank, giving you energy to do what you want to do? Can you occasionally place the food on an attractive plate instead of eating out of a carton? How about chewing the food slowly so you can really taste and savor the good work it is about to do for your health? Treat yourself and your meal as you would a friend, by giving it your complete attention. How many of us continually eat on the run or carry that "on the run energy" to a meal even when the meal doesn't need to be fast-paced? Sometimes, you may even want to light a candle and enjoy soft music.

If you have a family pet, you know the importance of walking the dog or providing the cat with a place to climb, sharpen its claws, and jump. We lovingly provide these necessities for our pets, but do you look upon your own self with the same love by providing yourself with the exercise you need? How about getting a little movement into your day? Can you get out at work on your break or lunch to take a walk and get some fresh air? How about after dinner? Being active has many health benefits, moving energy through you and leaving you better able to concentrate. "Better able to concentrate" got me off the couch. I wanted better mental clarity. You don't need to purchase any equipment. Just walk! I first walked around one block, then around two blocks, and from there I continued to expand my distance. Slowly, I was able to walk more comfortably without being winded. There are many forms of exercise; some cost nothing and some are expensive. People should follow their own energy. Put one foot out and try something enlivening and new.

Once, a man was kind to himself as he was fighting an illness. He got rid of negative things (people, emotions, and habits) and replaced them with uplifting ones. He watched comedies to make himself laugh and pick up his mood. It worked, and he was able to successfully navigate his illness into recovery because he found ways to be kind to himself.

Do you give yourself a quiet healing space away from negativities to nurture your soul, or are you constantly running and doing errands? Slow down and breathe every once in awhile. I feel the human-race in general does not allow this. We keep striving to go and go. It is like our finish line keeps getting moved further away each time we get close to reaching it. How unfair we can be to ourselves! In a real race, if the finish line got moved each time we advanced to it, we would protest to the judges. Yet in real life, how many times we reach our destination, whether mentally or physically, and we already are figuring out our next errand, without ever enjoying where we just arrived? Our finish line has indeed moved on us, yet we continue to allow this unfair race.

Sometimes we even race to wait. Please reread that. We race to wait. We are becoming a society of should-have-been-there-or-had-it-yesterdays. When we are in a hurry mentally, our bodies can't help but feel the rhythm. Think of Thanksgiving. We barely spend a day giving thanks for all we have before we are quickly participating in the next holiday by shopping for the "gotta-haves." Black Friday marks the start of the Christmas season and is really fun and economical for most, but Black Friday gets earlier each year—now there's Black Thursday! I know there are many good sales on Black Thursday, but I feel with all certainty that they will still be there on Fabulous Finds Friday, Slamming Saturday, Hot Sale Sunday, or Madness Monday. My soul deflates as once again the race is on. It is the same feeling I got years ago when some banks began opening on Sunday. I also feel with all certainty that people who don't get their banking done on Sunday can pick one of the other six days to accomplish it. Every business has an angle or a market strategy. The market is playing into our frenzy, and we are hooked more than ever. I am not old fashioned, but I feel we have launched ourselves into constant propulsion instead of enjoying the space we are sitting or standing in during the present. Are we losing a sense of sacredness, a space for rest, or just plain old simplicity? Where in life are you buying into the idea of move, move, move? Is it a building or just in your mind? Uninterrupted hours allow you to slow down to just be, regroup your thoughts, or heal. This can allow you to be satisfied with what is, while being eager for what is coming.

Continue your quest for self-respect and confidence. Get counseling to build your self-esteem. Learn how to have self-confidence because then others will respect you, too. When you stand up for yourself by holding onto that confidence and self-esteem, others will not be able to deny giving you the same. Let go of behaviors that deep down you know aren't healthy because guilt will erode your self-respect. Leave abusive situations. Don't let others use you, and insist others treat you with respect. This is the best way to become a true friend to you. Encourage yourself daily. Give yourself the pep talk you'd give a friend or a stranger. The more you are motivated by love, the more fearless and free your actions will become. Wouldn't you like to be a fearless, loving, and confident person? Gain your self-confidence by loving yourself.

You may be tired of your way of life, but you don't need to stop living and loving. Maybe all you need to do is look for new ways to express that love into your own everyday living. You are always changing and learning about yourself, but staying centered to your core with love never has to change. LET YOUR PRESENT TO YOURSELF BE YOUR PRESENCE. Stay as connected to yourself as you can, and don't abandon yourself as if you were your worst enemy. Keep your air mask handy, and embrace yourself over and over again!

There are further ideas and examples in the titled "Health and Other Snippets" chapter.

> *"Affirming positively is a memory
> and heart whisper."*
> —Renee Salvatori

Affirmations

Affirmations mean confirming and asserting what you already know. Maybe your consciousness does not remember, but your subconscious is very aware of how wonderful you are. Affirming is combining the conscious and the subconscious. This is a way to support and agree with all parts of yourself. Affirmations are like a personal cheering section or a pat on the back, so you should use them each and every day. They are very easy and quite fun. Write your affirmations—or sweet words to yourself—on index cards, and place them in areas that you will see, like a bathroom mirror, refrigerator door, in front of a toilet, behind a toilet, in front of a sink, or even on the steering wheel. Use your imagination.

If you combine your affirmation statements with *"I AM"* statements, they are very powerful. You have survived your past and have gone through resistances and previous training to become this person you see in the mirror today. Affirm all this goodness to yourself. Look in the mirror and tell yourself, "I AM A MIRACLE." Here are some examples of "I am" statements that are my favorites.

"I am" courage
"I am" enough!
"I am" willing
"I am" purpose

"I am" divinely protected
"I am" not alone
"I am" smart
"I am" health
"I am" a good person
"I am" love
"I am" strength
"I am" direction
"I am" financially sound
"I am" okay
"I am" happiness
"I am" wisdom
"I am" grounded
"I am" inner peace
"I am" trust
"I am" worthy
"I am" light
"I am" the whole package
"I am" a good mother (father)
"I am" a good wife (husband)
"I am" a good daughter (son)
"I am" making great progress towards all my goals

You may also view these "I am" affirmations as using the name of God to help you tap into spiritual power. The name God revealed to Moses was, "I am that I am." It also means, "as above, so below." "I am here below that which I am above," or "As God is in heaven, so God is on earth with me." Right here, where you are, is where God resides. God is a pulse of energy that resides in every soul.

So if I were to say, "I am sick," "I am tired," "I am having a good day," or "I am healthy," I positively or negatively tap into my spiritual power. It can also become my reality, as spoken words command energy. Sure, there are still days that I wake up and say, "Man, am I tired," but I try to add, "But I'll be better in a little while." I am still honest enough with myself to admit that I am tired, but I am also trying to create my upcoming reality.

Some of my daily notes to myself have been: *I am loved. You look beautiful. Breathe! I thrive everywhere I turn. Smile! Did you hug yourself yet? What can I do for you today? You are safe and protected. Did you get your little rest today? I always prosper. I know in which direction to go.* Again, use your imagination. These statements are your own little psychological team. If you can drop the "wrong" thought, then you can lose the problem. Start creating a new and improved you, and keep cheering yourself on. Change your affirmations often and mix them up. After a few weeks, they lose their punch and can simply become habit. Try this energy, and see if it influences your body. If you have many years of negative feedback in yourself, it may take some conscious and diligent effort to affirm positively. You can merge both the conscious and unconscious parts. These "I am" statements can even be done with focused and intentional breathing for a bigger impact.

*"If we learned and used Lamaze
or labor breathing techniques,
we could birth a whole new us."*
—Renee Salvatori

Breathing

We breathe in and out about 23,000 times a day because all our body's cells need oxygen to stay alive. Have you ever babied along a small pit fire by fanning it so it has oxygen to grow? Our bodies work in much the same way. We can fuel our bodies with lots of good oxygen; we need the oxygen inside to ignite us. It carries through to all our internal workings and to every cell, gland, and organ. When you breathe deep and long or slow and gently, you hook your body up to its natural rhythm. Oxygen is to the body what gasoline is to a vehicle.

Breathing is responsible for 99 percent of our entire oxygen and energy supply. Poor breathing worsens health issues like asthma, stress, obesity, and many other maladies. Breathing literally dictates our lifespan. In general, we do not take in enough oxygen. We don't have to buy it in a bottle or package, yet we don't utilize it to its fullest. God has worked out a great recycling plan for our breathing. The trees and plants take in the carbon dioxide we exhale and exchange it for pure oxygen we inhale. It is free. A new invention on the market today is the Breathslim, which has scientific studies backing up its results. It teaches you how to breathe more efficiently. Just twenty minutes a day can increase oxygen intake by 24 percent, diminish snoring, resolve sleep problems, decrease food cravings, normalize metabolism and increase fat burning, and improve health and well-being. Even without the scientific backing of a training tool like the Breathslim, the evidence pointing out the benefits of a good oxygen supply is amazing. Whatever ways we choose to increase our oxygen intake will benefit us many times over.

Have you ever watched a baby breathe? Babies breathe with their abdomens. As we age, our breath starts to leave us. We become affected by our stresses, life styles, and environments. We even hold our breath when we are stressed. After breathing like this over time, our bodies learn this habit and the diaphragm gets stuck and stays in this hindered state. Older people's breathing is very shallow and looks as if their breathing is in their throats. Breathing deep and low, from the abdomen, is the ideal way. We can relearn by starting at our chest area and working down. Fully extend your lungs and diaphragm so that the breath appears to be raising the stomach. Our diaphragm is a strong, thin muscle partition between the chest and the abdomen, and it acts like a bellows which pushes oxygen throughout. Take in a few good deep breaths and see how far you can expand that area. Now that it is in your consciousness, you may want to practice this technique anytime.

Deep breathing is good for stress, meditation, affirmations, and overall health. When we have pain, we breathe by shallow breaths. This is the time to really breathe deep intentionally. When my children hurt themselves, I always remind them to breathe deep, as it makes the pain less intense. Again, it has scientifically proven benefits. A few years ago, I started to notice that I would hold my breath or breathe shallow when nervous. I would also tense my pelvic and buttocks muscles. The funny thing is that when you are stressed, you need to relax and breathe. Notice how you breathe. When does your breathing go deep? Is it when you are feeling relaxed? When does your breath become shallow? Is it traffic, being around a certain person, or a certain situation? Notice what stops your breath, and try to start it again.

If I am running late and feeling tense, I try to remember to do deep breathing. I will do this in the shower, shaving, blow drying my hair, and getting dressed. It is super easy to do but very hard to remember to do it. Try to breathe in calm and breathe out calm. This can be done in a car, bus, a bathroom stall, before meditations, or lying in bed. There is one warning though. If this breathing makes you lightheaded, please do not do this while driving. I tried this at a time when I was so deficient in oxygen and so overflowing with stress that I almost passed out. So please, use caution if it has been a while since you have done deep belly-breathing. Your body may not know what to do with all the oxygen it is now getting. Here is another fun warning. When you are lying in bed, deep breathing can put you to sleep peacefully.

There is also breathing and imagery. Breathe in positive statements and breathe out negative statements. Visualize as you breathe. Here is how it is done: Breathe in peace, breathe out stress. Breathe in love, breathe out anger. Breathe in health, breathe out sickness. Breathe in love, breathe out jealousy. Breathe in harmony, breathe out disharmony. All positives should be on the in breath and all negatives on the out breath. Pick one and try it. Do a few of these until you feel your body start to relax, and then switch to positives on both the in and the out breaths. It will be like this; breathe in peace, breathe out peace. Breathe in love, breathe out love. Breathe in health, breathe out health. Breathe in calm, breathe out calm.

Breathe for relaxation and health. Oxygen is an amazing life force and in our breathing we continue to exist.

"What you think, will be."
—Renee Salvatori

Worthiness

"Worthiness" can hold a positive or a negative feeling, depending on how you feel. We are all worthy, each and every one of us, but few of us believe in our own worthiness. Your own worthiness is something you feel or allow. It is given or taken away only by you. God loves you unconditionally and will not take this love away. We are the ones who limit our own worthiness. Realizing we are unconditionally worthy is such a valuable gift, but it is up to us, individually, to open and utilize this gift.

Some people have a hard time receiving the gift. They feel the need to suffer themselves into worthiness, and if they haven't suffered enough, they are not really worthy. In truth, there does not need to be any suffering or disallowing. We are already worthy enough! Suffering has a negative connotation, but the word *worthiness* needs to have a positive connotation, along with words like "allowing," "willing," "purely loving," and "believing." There is a saying that for those who believe, no proof is necessary and for those who don't believe, no proof is possible. Can you believe in your own worthiness, and begin to make your definition of worthiness a positive one?

For whatever reason, I never felt I had earned or even deserved worthiness. I wasn't special enough, or I had never "done enough" to deserve it. One day, while I was at a Reiki session, I felt worth ever so deeply! I felt surround by a beautiful energy; I not only felt it shining on me but also from within me. It was as if saying, "Welcome to the light of your worthiness. What took you so long?" I felt light. The best way I can explain it is like a child who struggled for years to understand a mathematics concept then to unexpectedly grasp it. Who really understands why or how realizations or concepts are gained, but I understood an important lesson on that day. I felt excited to start enjoying life again. It was my "Ah-Ha" moment. I realized I was the one blocking my own worthiness, and I was indeed as worthy as everyone else. I felt as if I literally walked out of a dark cave and into the sunlight of unconditional worthiness. I cried tears of release as I became willing to begin to allow it. Don't shut yourself in somewhere and refuse to see your worthiness and light. Claim what is yours.

You are the one who has to feel and allow worthiness. We may tell a Venus-like beauty she is beautiful, but unless *she* truly feels she is beautiful, she will not be beautiful. We may try to convince a king he really is a ruler of a region, but if he doesn't believe he is king, he will not rule like a king. I can tell you that you are worthy, but unless *you* really believe in yourself and feel your worth, you will not experience worthiness. Realize that the only permission needed for worthiness is your own! You don't need anyone else's approval for this wonderful feeling. When you get that true sense of worthiness, you, too, may even shed a happy tear.

Allowing may not come overnight. It may be a process of allowing, as the realization sets in. For me, it was like I was in a big cardboard box. I peeped out a small crack to see my worthiness light, and then I lifted the first lid flap. As I got more comfortable, I lifted another flap. I did not open all the flaps at once; it was a slow and cautious process. I was working at letting the light in though. Even today, I am still in the process of realizing my full worthiness. Don't wait until tomorrow to look for your light. Don't put off tomorrow what you can do today. Start feeling that sun on your face now.

Being willing to feel and believe is not the end, however. We must now do something. Start to enjoy you. Start to enjoy your life, your car, your home, and all the wonderful things you have. Do you feel worthy to enjoy all your comforts and all the wonderful things that come your way? How about really enjoying that nice easy chair in your living room? Do you feel worthy to sit down and enjoy it? Do you feel worthy to pamper yourself with something you have wanted to do or see? Can you love yourself in your true worthy fashion? Are you worthy of health? Do you value yourself enough to give yourself down time, vitamins, and good food? You are worth your worthiness.

Stay aware, as sometimes you can sabotage feelings of worthiness. How many times have you hesitated to start a new venture or a different avenue of living because of feeling unworthy? Maybe someone convinced you that you didn't deserve the change. Maybe you became a victim of the same motto that most do, "You have to work hard to have nice things or make a living." Maybe working just comes easy to you and maybe so does your financial flow, but you won't accept it because you didn't have to work hard for it. You associate worthiness with hard work. This can sound silly, but it does happen. You may also be stuck in a low-paying job, not because of employment opportunities, but because you do not feel worthy of a better one.

Ego also has the ability to self-sabotage as does low self-esteem, which doesn't always have the appearance of slumped shoulders, puppy eyes, or in the corner hovering. Both can be closely linked to feeling unworthy. You know the saying; "You" can't judge a book by its cover"? True self-esteem and confidence, which are neither shy nor boisterous, are indicators of allowing our true worthiness. When you love someone, you want the best for that person. When we start loving ourselves, then we want the best for ourselves too. That best is believing and allowing our own worthiness. Self-esteem and worthiness are synonymous.

Here is another self-sabotage: How about refusing to be happy, healthy, or financially secure because you don't want to out-worthy anyone else? You may refuse to have a better life than your parents did because you don't want to outshine them. You feel they are more worthy than you are because they are your parents. Don't you want your children to have a better or more fulfilling life than you do? The thoughts of your parents should never hold you back from your own advancement and worthiness. They want you to shine in your own birthright. Your birthright is to accept your worthiness for all the goodness it holds.

Sometimes it is this shining of ourselves that leaves us feeling vulnerable and hiding. We are afraid of our wonderful selves. Every being has such a gift of strength, compassion, skills, or just the ability to smile ourselves into the energy of earth. We are all light extending from God, and we are meant to extend this light and enjoy doing so. Sometimes we are frightened and frozen by the light instead of the dark. This action does seem backwards but happens just the same, many times over. In this backwardness, we cannot move forward fully into our integrated self. We are each fantastic and should not be afraid to let it show. Not only giving it to others, but giving it to our very selves by living it out. Give yourself the right to live fully without hiding in the dark shadows of feeling undeserving.

Most people talk of Constitutional rights and freedoms and will fight for them. Do you fight for allowing your own rights and liberty of self? Can you be your own ambassador of good will or your own agent of relief of darkness. Your hiding or denying your internal freedoms keeps you from fully joining in life. Free yourself and in doing so, you will liberate others to do the same. Shine your light and pass the symbolic torch on to another. We are all worthy and deserving. Become willing to allow…all!

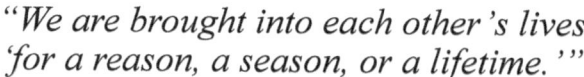

"We are brought into each other's lives for a reason, a season, or a lifetime."
—Ram Dass

Relationships

I originally had much to say on relationships, maybe because I was overanalyzing this very human part of living, but I have limited myself to a few thoughts. Relationship to self has been addressed more thoroughly in the chapters *Be Kind to Yourself* and *Mirror Help*. This chapter will also discuss relationship with others.

If any relationship, whether with a lover, family member, work associate, PTA group, or church (you get the idea), makes you feel devalued, belittled, or neglected, it's time to do some investigating. We all know life is too short to be spent feeling bad. How others treat us is very connected to how we relate to ourselves. Our inner feelings of self-worth, confidence, and love are mirrored back to us by how we allow others to treat us.

So many times people stay longer than necessary in relationships because they lack confidence or are merely relieved to find a relationship, even socially, to participate in. We bargain quietly in our minds or loudly with others to stay in these relationships. We even exchange our true inner spirit for this blighted connection to others. If a relationship is not filling your soul, you could be starving, just as if you were starving for food.

If any relationship is not a give and take, then it is only a servant and a mastership. Have you become a slave to another, even if only mentally? We cannot make others happy if they are unhappy, no matter how good our intentions are. On the other hand, others cannot make us happy if we are unhappy, no matter how much attention or material goods they give us.

Relationships have to come from the inside, not the outside.

Your love and peace depend on analyzing the relationship with yourself first. Cleaning up your internal turmoil is key to finding out why your relationship is struggling or why the momentum of failure follows you. Like a person who quits every job because he is unhappy, until he understands what exactly he is looking for in a job and names it, no job will ever be fulfilling. The same is true in relationships. After the personal inner turmoil is smoothed out, all relationships will get better and better. It's as though you've made the perfect domino train; you will be aligning that first domino to all the others and then setting that first domino in motion. That first push is the love you feel for yourself. You now understand what you want and need and how not to sell yourself short. You know yourself and you can adhere to Shakespeare's line, "To thy own self be true."

If you are having difficulty navigating some areas of relationships, seek help to build your self-esteem and find your strengths. Reading this book is a wonderful start! Once you understand yourself, knowing who you are, exactly what you want, and where you aim on going, you will attract compatible companions in all areas. The more at ease we become with ourselves, the more peacefully and agreeably others will respond in kind. Also, the more self-esteem we have, the more confidence we will gain from others. We can't block out the world, so we must keep incorporating understanding of self and others. We learn from all our relationships, healthy and unhealthy ones. While we are learning about ourselves and finding our true colors, others can help refine us from a rough diamond into a recognizable gem.

Another area to consider is how you allow others to speak to you. How do your children talk back to you, whatever their ages? How about your work associates, parents, spouse, people you see daily, and your own inner voice? Do you sugarcoat another's life so he doesn't have to adjust his own sour taste? I have a friend whose husband had a bad home life and is still angry over the past. He yells and demeans her often. She accepts this because she explains his past was bad and he needs peace now. So this lovely lady allows his mistreatment towards her instead of making him be accountable for his today. We cannot continue to take on other pains, insecurities, mistreatments, and excuses. If we do, we become nothing more than a punching bag. We can't make other's lives right, and we can't do their work for them.

Have you ever heard the statement, "You are the greatest person in the world, just like everyone else"? We are all great, and we are all learning great lessons. Souls are drawn together again and again for personal soul development. Our work is not to fix others but to understand ourselves. Try not to let your joy be determined by others' good or bad experiences. You must not judge another's personal lessons as your failure or your reward; just focus on *your* lessons and learn them with confidence.

Life is an interaction with each person performing his own part, and we may need to give others their parts back. Here are some examples I will share. My niece was hesitating to turn in her two-week notice to a job in which she was not happy. Her fear was that the supervisor would be angry and be put out, so she was willing to stay miserable to appease her boss. She needed to focus on her own feelings of job happiness and not the happiness of the supervisor. One year, I fretted over planning a vacation. I felt the memories of previous years that went wrong pushing down on me.

The times the condo was dirty, the town had nothing to do, or the weather didn't cooperate, and the list went on. I agonizingly searched through many vacation lodging sites and almanacs hoping to make this one perfect. It was drudgery until one wise person explained that I just couldn't take it all upon myself? To make everyone's vacation perfect was an endless task. So what if things did not go perfectly, and what if it rained, or the town didn't offer the recreation wanted? I needed to find my own comfort with it while others found their own ways of dealing with it.

We are not here to make others' lives right. We are not their designated Guardian Angel. Some may hesitate to take a part at first, but they will adjust to their new roles. We can begin to direct the energy of others who come our way by becoming the director of our own plays—our lives. We can yell, "Cut!", "Retake!", and "That's a wrap!" whenever we feel it is necessary. If you do not spend time analyzing a tough relationship and where it is at the present, the same mistakes may be repeated again and again in later relationships.

Whatever answers you find to your questions, try not to surround them in judgment. There is no right and wrong or good and bad; they are just answers. What does "just answers" mean to you? Throughout life, friends and lovers come and go. We are constantly changing, and so are others. Some float in and out of our lives like an autumn breeze, others linger like a winter freeze, some feel like the newness of spring, while others feel like summer's warmth on our face. There is a season for everything and everyone. You can be with the most perfect of perfect partners but if it isn't what one of you are wanting, it isn't going to work. I let a three year relationship end as I realized his and my dreams were taking us down different roads. We were both perfect for each other, but it was the timing that wasn't.

I will lovingly say this: There should be no guilt if you need to stay in a relationship for your well-being, protection, security, or food. However, if the relationship is abusive, run. A relationship with a parent, guardian, or spouse may need to be respectfully endured for a time. In the meantime, try to build your self-esteem and continue to nurture yourself in ways that will benefit you not only now, but later as well. This will give you the fortitude to propel yourself into your new life adventure. The self-esteem and confidence you work on will keep you from being taken back into those earlier times.

Role models, like the famous baseball player you once wanted to be or the singer whose clothes and mannerisms you emulated, are the quiet little bonds no one else may ever know you carry in your mind or heart. As we age, we drop some role models and adopt new ones. It may be time to analyze who you are still holding in the sacred places of your heart and mind. Older does not always mean wiser! Are your current role models internally propelling you to your mental best or highest thoughts? They should be. If you get to imagine and pretend in your day dreams, pick a really uplifting and inspiring person to admire and "be."

Life is ongoing adventures with many purposeful relationships which can either help us discover who we really are or hide who we really are, even from ourselves. The bottom line is, relationships should never make you or others feel inferior, and one should never play games with others' minds and hearts. The famous saying, "Do unto others as you want done unto you" is still a Golden Rule. Not only does it feel nice to be treated with love, but it is also nice to treat others with love.

And don't forget to have that purposeful relationship with yourself, too!

> *"Stand your ground and the ground
> will help you stand."*
> —Renee Salvatori

Have an Opinion of Your Own

I can't stand it when someone—a parent, grandparent, church figure, older child, spouse—wants to convince me he knows what is best for me and will not let me have my own opinion. It is stifling because my own creativity suffers. Maybe that person has a hunch about what is good for you but to push his hunch on you means he is not only living his life, but yours, too, and as we saw in the last section, we must all direct our own lives. Each of us is a free-willed being. We get to live our lives, make mistakes, and make our own memories. The only life you should live is your own, and that means having your own thoughts and opinions and contributing to your own outcome.

So often we sacrifice our integrity by shaping our decisions and behaviors around what we feel others will want of us, rather than by being true to ourselves. We sell our souls and cave into others' wants. Don't keep trying to please everybody by saying or doing what you feel will make them happy. You can never give another person enough goodness to truly make him happy. He may feel satisfied for a moment, but he will continually look to you to say and do what he needs in order for his happiness gauge to stay at "full." Other people's happiness has to come from deep within themselves. If you don't let people know their happiness cannot come from you, then you will never be done making others happy. You will die before you find your own happiness because you will be too busy trying fruitlessly to find others' happiness for them.

Open Your Heart to the True You

Focus on your own happiness, thoughts, and creative opinions; go by that old saying, "Don't try so hard to fit in when you were born to stand out." It's never good to have a belligerent opinion, but an honest-to-goodness opinion you feel deep within your heart is much to be desired. You think and feel, research and listen, to create opinions that are your own, based on your own personality. Your opinions allow you to stand in your own power, refusing to let others stifle your truths. Others may try to "guilt" you into doing and believing their beliefs and opinions. They may not directly and overtly tell you how to think or feel, but they may slyly try to get control by using guilt. Society, institutions, schools, religions, family, spouses, and friends have all been successful at using this destructive manipulation. How about a father who casually mentions that he never got to play a certain sport and is looking forward to his son playing since he never got to? Perhaps the son does not wish to play that sport. How about many who state that church is needed in order to be saved? This guilt indoctrination holds you there by fear. Years ago I decided that my two children needed to go from home school to a public school. The backlash I received from some in my local group was heavy. Their responses were, "How could you do this? It is the parents' obligation and right to teach their children." I cried as I knew that the timing was right to put them into another school setting, but the guilt felt was so heavy that I needed to go speak to someone about it. I worked though feeling like a failure and sent them to another school. I was amazed to find out that one of the mothers who criticized me so harshly had herself sent three of her own children to a school a year later. Had I continued to home school because of guilt over another's opinion, I would have been very angry to learn later that another did exactly what I desired and longed to do a year earlier; it would have been anger at the other person but even more-so at myself for allowing another to change me. Other types of guilt indoctrination can run so deep that you may need time to reprogram and recover.

Some people are just so easygoing and compliant. When asked what they want to do or where they want to go, they will always say, "It doesn't matter." Does this sound like you? Go ahead; give an opinion every once in a while on little things, or you may find it has been so long since you cared that you've forgotten how to give an opinion. If asked where you want to eat, make a choice and be happy you contributed, even if you really do not care. If asked what movie you want to watch, pick one every once in a while, and feel the satisfaction of gifting your opinion.

Once you recognize your own power, you will see the true you blossom, and your identity will sharpen. The people you struggle with will either fall into place around you or fall away from you, just as the creative you falls into place around or away from them. Everybody just is, and everyone needs to be his own somebody. Being a "somebody" does not only mean doing things, but also having your own opinions and creativity. You are creating yourself and will be contributing to life as everyone else is. You matter in life, and you make a difference.

No one should ever have to justify his existence, experience, or opinions to another. Everyone deserves to live his own life. Stand for what you believe. Stay true to your own opinions and thoughts. You can always change them if and when you need or are ready to change. Have fun creating and recreating from your own "noggin of creativity." No one knows more about you than you yourself. Don't let others convince you otherwise. It takes courage to stand out and have your own opinion, but remember, they are they, and you are you.

"Be who you are and be that well."
—Abraham Lincoln

Individuated

Having your own opinions and being an individual sound like the same thing, but they are different, like a set of twins. The twins may look exactly the same, but they are two separate individuals living their own lives. They will be very close, but they still remain two distinct people. They may or may not hold the same opinions about politics, schools, music genres, or any other subject. They have a connection, but the connection does not control their very beings. Being individuated and having your own opinions are both very important, but they are different.

Have you ever heard of a parent making her child play a certain sport because the parent is living her own life through that child? The child may hate the sport (opinion), but the parent won't allow the child to quit, as the parent cannot distinguish (individuate) the body of the child from her own. A person should never intend to live her life through the lives of others. We are all individuals and should never be restricted or guilted into living the life of another, whether that other person is our parent, spouse, friend, or other person. It is too difficult to be someone you're not. Learn the process of being an individual.

Years ago, I was lamenting that the umbilical cord was still so attached between myself and my mother. I cried that I just wanted to be more separate from her! A very wise person carefully explained to me that we never want to be separate as that is a lonely thing; we only want individuation. We are humans, and we all need each other. If the relationship is abusive, then you need to separate yourself for protection. But to be separated from healthy individuals denies us this piece of humanity. I needed my mother, but I also needed my own individuality. You, too, may need to figure out how to gain your individuality if someone is living through you. This may be hard if living according to the wishes and desires of another has been your habit for years.

Stand up and be counted! There is no one like the individual you. We want to be connected to the big picture but still hold onto our own pictures to remain healthy. It's a balance. We humans are like pack animals. We all have longings to be in a social group, tribe, or pack. We need each other to survive and thrive. Look inside a pack of dogs, and you will see great diversity as each dog stands in its own power. One will be the alpha dog, one the mothering leader, one the food supplier, and yet another pack babysitter. All have their specific jobs, but all are still connected to form a whole. We do not want to be separated from our pack. We just want to be individuated.

Look deeply into your eyes and acknowledge that you truly are an individual. Do not try to separate; try only to individuate. You can share others' garden space, but plant your own seeds of choice. One gardener may plant tomatoes, and another may plant carrots, while you plant strawberries. How boring if we all planted tomatoes! How boring if we were all mere extensions of another! We moved our hand to scratch our head because they told us to. We sat to eat when the other was hungry. Our scratching and eating would be based on another's living needs and expectations. *Know* who you are, and *be* who you are. It is not only knowing, but also being. *Be the individual you.*

Another area that stifles our own individuality (individuated) is comparing ourselves to others. Comparison is the thief of joy. Man is the only creature who refuses to be what he is. Can you imagine seeing a cat trying to be a dog? How about a fish trying to be a bird? "You" trying to be a "them" or a "them" trying to be a "you"? When this happens, we cross the boundary of our own being. There is a saying that goes something like; if a fish analyzed itself against its inability to climb a tree then it would definitely be a loser. Comparing will always make us a loser in ourselves.

You may say, "But isn't the act of comparing a healthy thing?" I feel comparing has its time and place. Growing up and comparing ourselves to our classmates, social groups, and neighbors is a very natural and fundamental process of youth. This is how we start to learn our places and what types of actions are acceptable in certain settings. But, as in all things, we grow up and close that chapter of our life. There should come a time in life when we no longer have to compare ourselves to others because we have started to become more comfortable with and in ourselves. The mime in the mirror doesn't need to exist past childhood and young adulthood. We eventually need to give up comparisons. Masquerading as someone else will only create frustration.

Use others for inspiration, but never live in their shadow. Free up your thoughts for your own creativity and individuality. People talk about "keeping up with the Jones" for a reason. We all have done it. Our neighbor buys a new vehicle, so we long to buy a new vehicle. We may wish we had someone's house or family dynamics. When we wish in this way, or envy others by comparing ourselves to them, we stifle the true us. We become them. Can you imagine if everyone did exactly as the person in front of them did? It would be like a continual game of follow the leader. Picture a checkerboard with all the red and black playing pieces going to the same squares in a follow-the-leader style. It would be repetitive and boring. To have a truly fun game of life, we all need our own moves. We need to go to our own squares and play our own game. You may not have been born a Jones; you may have been born a Smith. Both are equally refreshing and important.

Just as no two snowflakes are exactly the same; no two people are exactly the same. Together we all make a wonderful snow-covered landscape. Trust that you are becoming the beautiful individual soul you have come to earth to be. You are you, and nothing is any better than that. Do you remember the "I am" affirmation statements? Try these: "I am an individual," "I am unique," and "It's easy to be me." We have all been given free will to become who we are and to think how and what we want to think. Do not give it away consciously or unconsciously. Be individuated, not separated. In the words of Shakespeare, "To thy own self be true."

> *"If you control anyone or anything other than you, that is not control, that is manipulation and judgment, in the highest form."*
> —Renee Salvatori

Control and Judgment

You can only control one thing: yourself. Even then there are times that people control too much of themselves. When one tries to control every part of life and living, that is considered micro-managing. Micro is very minute or small, and manage is to treat with care or alter with manipulation. So ask yourself, are you one who treats others with care or alters life with manipulation in big or small ways? In micro-managing, the spontaneity of living and life are taken away because of too much manipulating and altering of details. This can create an undue burden on you and others because each and every action is watched and perhaps judged. If you feel you have to control conditions in order to feel good or be happy, you are stifling your own and most likely others' ability to feel good. The judgment component is a very real and big issue that many do not even realize happens because it is all done on such an unconscious level; unknowingly, one begins to judge his ability to make things happen or not make things happen. The outcome is judged either well or badly. Control and judgment may not only be synonymous but can become a cycle.

Some people look at control as simply being very proactive in their lives. In being too proactive, they take every measure possible in trying to manage a well-planned outcome. Excessive planning can take out all the excitement of any activity and make it a burden. You want to plan but not over-plan. Some look at not trying to control anything as letting "God's will be done" and they completely turn their planning over to God as if God were to even fold and place their clothing in a suitcase for them. Others go through life haphazardly as free spirits. Both of these types are extremes and not necessarily good. If you plan on going to college one day or taking a special trip somewhere, you should be saving some money and working on a schedule to accomplish your plans. You'll be doing your part in preparing for that day, but you won't need to control every detail. You can even ask God for support and guidance.

We should prepare and be proactive but not excessively controlling because over-control only makes you and others around you miserable. No one can control everything. Think of a rope during tug-of-war. Eventually, one side must let go, just as we must learn to let go of the rope when we have no control. We can softly be while others softly are. Being soft is not tugging tightly in life.

Are you concerned with where you are at all times? It keeps you stuck in controlling the next second, minute, hour, day, week, month, and year. When this happens, you cannot flow softly with the energy surrounding you. Controlling circumstances and events only hardens your energy with undue responsibility which you have no control over. Imagine energy that is hard, and then imagine the soft energy of just being. Can you feel the difference when you feel yourself with soft energy and then feel yourself with hard energy? When you find the soft spot, energy just opens up. Just be! As in the Beatles song, "Let It Be," just let things be, no matter how you think it all should turn out. You can't control everything, and that's just the way it is. When you feel frustration over controlling something, it's usually because you are holding or pulling too tightly for an outcome you want. You are having trouble releasing the rope of micro-managing. Remember, micro-managing can slide you into judgment. Judgment gives off hard energy, whether it is judgment of others or judgment of your own abilities to control.

What about judgment of others? When we judge others, we send out little negative barbs into their energy fields. These small spikes block healing energies and may cause health disorders. Some gifted energy healers can actually watch these hooks being projected into others when judgment, criticism, and anger are directed. We inject these same barbs into ourselves with self-judgment. Judging is not the best alternative, especially when you or others need mercy and compassion. We do not want to be attached to negative situations through the judgment of others nor through the unconscious judgment of self. Think of judgment as a fishing hook attached to a fish. Depending on how big that fish and hook of judgment are, they can pull you along in endless and random directions. How important is landing that big one? Judgment's after effects can head us in a direction that is not desirable or toward the slippery slope of self-pity.

Can you think of things you try to control but can't? Here are some I've learned people can't control:

You can't control whether or not you or your children get sick. You can feed yourself and your family well, take vitamins, and get enough sleep, but sometimes, even with the best intentions, you or they will still get sick. Do you then judge yourself as a bad parent or a bad person for letting the kids or yourself get sick?

You can't control the rain; you can only wear a rain coat. You may judge the rain as a nuisance because it is coming when you don't want it or not coming when you do, but nature rains when she needs to rain; she doesn't rain or withhold rain just to inconvenience you.

You can't control the sun; you can only dress lighter or find shade. Because you can't control the atmosphere's thermostat, you may judge the heat or cold as unnecessary as well as uncomfortable, though the extreme temperatures may be needed to grow crops or make viruses dormant.

You can't control how others interact with you; you can only be who you are. If others don't like you, do you judge yourself based on how they feel about you? Do you allow them to have their own opinion as you, in spite of their thoughts, softly go through your day?

You can prepare wholesome meals but you can't control what your children eat or if they are hungry. You may judge them as stubborn if they don't eat what you think they should. You can only control what you are hungry for or if you are even hungry at all. You can't control your child's interests and ambitions. What if your child doesn't want to take a certain class, but you feel the class will enhance his life later? Do you judge your child lazy because of his own desires?

You can't control other drivers. A driver drives past you quickly, and you judge him as stupid while he thinks of himself as fun. You can't control how anyone drives; you can only control how you do.

You can't control how others choose to decorate their homes. You see a house decorated in a fashion that does not appeal to you. You take your judgmental notes of how you think it should be. You have taken their ability to decorate for themselves and mentally made their home yours. You can control how you decorate your house, but that is all.

You can't control what others say and do. You observe or hear an interaction between people and you can't believe what is being said and done. In your mind, you start to imagine how their words and deeds should be playing out. But you must remember that everyone picks his own experiences in his own life classroom, so we need to keep from trying to attach our views to others' experiences.

Have you ever noticed how judgment creeps in when you hear news on television and you begin to feel ill, angry, or opinionated? You have your thoughts on how a country, business, or home should be run, but by staying actively attached to those ideas, you have taken away their power and tried to make it yours. Your thoughts of how things "should be" can easily be turned into judgment, and with those judgments, you have attached yourself to situations. When you do not agree with what is being done, you can only bless the situation and those involved and move yourself away from them. Leaving these situations relinquishes our control and frustration and lets us live in our own life without judgment. You cannot be living your own life while mentally living in or trying to fix someone else's life. To think that you know what's best for others, even if it is all done in love, can border on haughtiness. Knowing what is right for you is the only arena or classroom you should be in. If you start to feel judgment creep in, bless a situation or a person and move away.

We all have thoughts and preferences, but preferences are not judgment. A simple orange provides a clear example. You may not like oranges and move to another fruit section at the store, but if you judge the store negatively because it has too many varieties of oranges, then you are needlessly attaching yourself to that negative situation. Play with judgment throughout your day and see what kinds and degrees of judgment come up. Do your preferences cross over into judgment? How can you have your thoughts and preferences, yet stay unattached? You may laugh at some of the trivial and not so trivial ways you attach yourself to others or situations that arise during the day! You may even begin to see the humor in the judgment and control of yourself.

We can think of Helen Keller and how she navigated her life. Left blind and deaf by illness in her second year, she didn't have much control of many aspects in her life, and she had to go by instinct and trust—a true blind faith and trust. At first she tried to control what used to be and was angry and fearful until she learned to release resistance into soft easement. Maybe we should all have a little Helen Keller in us as we find our own ease and softness.

It can be terrifying to think you may lose control, but the truth is, while you may have had the illusion of control; you never had true control in the first place. You must cultivate the power to live fearlessly without manipulating or controlling. We control because fear of the "what if?" or fear of a mistake grips us. If a mistake is made, there is always a chance for a fresh start at any moment. Mistakes are not failures; they are only one way of learning how not to do something. Look around and see opportunity. What-if's and opportunities can both be positive. Control, judgment, and fear are emotions that wreak havoc when we hold on to them too tightly, and we truly don't need them if we are trying to feel good.

Giving up control does not mean surrendering or giving up. We are only giving up trying to manage and control every twist and turn in life, which only builds resistance anyway. We still need to steer our lives in the direction of our choosing. One cannot nor should not want to control and judge all the specifics in life, as this leaves no room for spontaneity. Being overly controlling is like wearing shoes that are much too tight; you have no wiggle room for your toes. Being in ease is only clothing yourself with a softness that allows resistance to fall away and harmonious energy to bathe your body. Allow fun and freshness without control and judgment. Take proactive steps each day to not control the uncontrollable.

"As seasoning is to your food, ego is to your soul. You just have to find the right balance."
—Renee Salvatori

Ego

I need to say something about ego because there has been so much written about it lately. I have read some great books on the subject and loved them. Ego can mean both the productive and counterproductive parts of your personality. Ego is like the little angel sitting on one of your shoulders and the little devil on the other. All of us work with this little angel and devil quandary. Ego is not necessarily bad or selfish; it just needs to be balanced. Ego is our personality and helps us take on ideas and interests for the betterment of ourselves and others. Ego can lead you forward to betterment, awareness, and newness in your life and that is all good. On the flip side, ego can also be overused, causing true clarity to become distorted and hindered. The ego learns and grows through life's experiences, trials, and errors. It can serve as a beacon or a hindrance.

Do understand that some ego is very beneficial. If we didn't have a little of the self/ego, we wouldn't have personalities. I finally understood when I was shaking off so much of the ego that I began to feel out of balance. I felt that all I was shaking off was taking my personality from me. I realized that some ego was needed to propel and motivate me forward. But where some people need to spice up their life with ego, others may need to strain some ego out. It is finding a harmonious balance.

Here are examples of when the ego may need straining. When you walk around feeling you are better than others, the ego needs to be checked. Be honest—are you the windbag in meetings or social gatherings because no one knows better than you? How do you feel when someone passes you on the road? Does your ego make you feel, how dare they? Do you always have to be right? Do you thrive on gossip because it inflates your own self-worth? Do you enjoy sarcasm because it inflates your value? Does the ego devil sitting on your shoulder convince you that you have to buy things to better yourself, when you financially do not have the funds? The need for pats on the back or constant accolades is an indicator that the ego needs some critiquing. An unbalanced ego can do a good bit of unnecessary and unproductive convincing!

An overactive ego is not always the problem, though. Here are examples of when the ego needs enhancement. Do you continually doubt yourself? Does your ego's voice accept your own divinity or does it tell you how little you are worth? Does it love you or does it run you down? Does your ego's voice sabotage you in other ways? To find the true balance, you may have to step back and look at yourself with fresh eyes. Picture the tiny devil on one shoulder and the tiny angel on the other. They are like positive and the negative currents. Both are beneficial, but you have to decide how to merge them successfully.

When you do things in your day without looking at the outcome as an ego-stoker, you are acting in pure love without ego attached; your actions are done entirely for the benefit of others. Egoless giving truly feels good. If I gave a gift or my time to an individual or to a club, but I only did it to make myself look good, then I am giving with strings—and my very big ego—attached. If, however, I gave a gift or my time without concern for how it made me look to others (including myself), I am not overly ego-based. I am acting genuinely with no strings or ego attached.

Keeping too small a belief in self is not humble. It is devastating. Having admiration for your excellence is not egotism, but bravery. When you appreciate yourself, you will always make forward progress. Do you view yourself as unique, and love yourself for your uniqueness, or are you being so modest that you have no opinion, zest, or life flowing through you? If you have no ego to propel you, you may want to add a dash of it to your life. If, on the other hand, you have an excess of ego, you may want to let go of the ego a bit.

"Never be afraid to try something new. Remember, amateurs built the ark, professionals built the Titanic."
—Frank Pepper

Belief Systems

Belief systems are values, ideas, or ways of living handed down or personally formed by self. They can be from anyone or anything in your life: parents, grandparents, past lives, teachers, friends, religion, books, a spouse or a significant other, or social groups. They can be simple beliefs ranging from which brand of cereal is best to more complex beliefs that incorporate years of your life, like your religious affiliation. Beliefs can be heartfelt or habit, something you have kept because you know no other way, you have no opinion, or you are inflexible about opening up to something new. Our beliefs can be comforting or disquieting. Each and every one of us must look into what our belief systems hold for us. Does it still serve you to believe others' truths or even some of your long-held truths of yesterday?

Here are a few examples of beliefs or truths that are held in different degrees. The first is from the Amish. Once married, an Amish man should not shave again. Amish women should never cut their hair as the Amish see women's hair as a crown from God. To the Amish, these customs are part of a very heartfelt belief system. In fact, one group of Amish "punished" another group for breaking community rules by tying them up, shaving the men, and cutting the women's hair. Those attacked were completely demoralized, and some said they would rather have been beaten. Personally, I'd rather have my hair cut. As most of us do, I willingly pay someone to cut my hair! We may not understand the belief systems of others, but nonetheless, these are very real beliefs which have been passed on from generation to generation.

What about the belief system that one has to marry someone from his own religious affiliation? What about marriage to someone of one's own race? How about only marrying someone from one's own social group? Not laughing so much now?

Let's go to some beliefs that are not so drastic but can be just as deeply ingrained. What about holiday traditions you have followed because someone passed on the tradition to you, but perhaps now those traditions just don't fulfill you or your family's needs or feel right and comforting to you anymore? How about having to name your child a family name because of culture, significance, or tradition? There is nothing wrong with following family traditions, if they feel right. If family traditions don't feel right, though, you need to evaluate beliefs in your system of being.

What about the believing you should be a certain type of father or mother based on your own parents behaviors? What if you wish to work outside the home, but your mother stayed home, so you believe that is what you should do? What if you want to stay home, but your mother worked outside the home, so you feel you should also work outside the home?

Here is another category of belief: work. Are you staying in a job you no longer enjoy because of a belief? I'm sure you've seen second-generation business people do exactly what their parents did because they believed they needed to carry on the family tradition, whether the family tradition was brick-layer or doctor. Again, there is nothing wrong in keeping family traditions and beliefs if they feel right; it is only when traditions feel restrictive and limiting that they should be reevaluated.

I read a story once of a granddaughter who cut off the top of the ham before she cooked it. She was the third generation to prepare ham this way. She finally asked her grandmother why all her family cooks followed this tradition. The grandmother replied that she'd never had a roasting pan deep enough to accommodate a whole ham and needed to cut some for the lid to fit snugly. Here is the interesting part: the grandmother's daughter and granddaughter both had roasting pans that could accommodate a big ham and still securely fasten the lid. For years, daughter and granddaughter had unnecessarily cut the ham. Unknowingly, we too may hold a belief or pattern that no longer pertains to us personally. Uncovering these beliefs may not be as simple as the example above, but it may start with just a simple question.

I have a personal example of a long-held belief; I believed all beeping sounds were serious, so serious that I became physically sick to my stomach on hearing one. One day I was presented with a peaceful opportunity to challenge why this happened. I was at a library feeling at peace when a steady beeping noise started. I wanted to bolt for the door, but I stayed and challenged myself. In my semi-quiet anxiety, I realized my anxiety stemmed from a very early memory from childhood when my brother was in the hospital. The beeps reminded me of his monitors. No wonder each time I was in the hospital birthing my babies or visiting family members, I would be in a state of massive nerves until I went home! Realizing the cause of my anxiety meant I no longer had to hold the beeps and trauma together. What if I hadn't challenged those simple beeps that day and had once again quickly left? All beeps would still subconsciously be affecting me today. This sounds so very simple and it was. The simple ones matter, too! Watch out for the bigger beliefs you may be stuck in, though. Stay present, as they may take more than a library trip to resolve.

The last set of beliefs I want to mention is the belief system you have about yourself. Do you believe you are unworthy, ugly, stupid, incapable, or too fat? Am I hitting a homerun here? Most of us have false beliefs lodged in our subconscious's, and even with some of the belief systems we hold due to family influences, the belief systems we hold against ourselves are and can be the hardest to challenge and heal. If you accept a limiting belief, it will become your reality. If you are looking for a reality check, challenge yourself by looking at your beliefs, large and small.

I subconsciously held a belief about the kind of person I was based on my interpretation of my parents' view of me. How many of us try so hard to make our parents proud of us? We try to be the perfect child and sometimes, no matter how hard we work at it, we believe we have failed. Our parents may not approve of something or may not give us the accolades we want, but this does not make us any less valuable. I remember one time believing the only right thing I did for my parents was giving them grandchildren. This belief was false, but it reflected where I was at that season in my life as much as if not more than any belief my parents held. Many of us base our beliefs about ourselves on what we believe others feel about us. My own father did this, too. We were filling out a question-and-answer book on his life and one of the questions was, how have you made your father proud? My father confided he felt he probably never made his father proud and believed he had failed as a son. Later, I took the book and went to talk with my grandfather. I asked him how my father made him proud. He looked at me with a sparkle in his eyes, and he replied he didn't know where to begin. As we talked, my grandfather told me many reasons he was proud of my dad.

Do you see how we unnecessarily hold beliefs of our inadequacies? We probably do make others proud, but our knowing this fact should not direct our inner beliefs about ourselves any more so than the feeling that we have failed others should. When we base our beliefs about ourselves on what others think, we keep mental and emotional energies locked. These beliefs need to be quickly abandoned because we are all wonderful! That is the belief to hold onto.

Casually challenge your beliefs rather than over-analyze them; listen and let challenges and new ideas start to flow through you. Why do I feel this way? When did I feel this way? What are my surrounding feelings or emotions? When you challenge a belief, one of two things will happen: you keep it, or you toss it. As in the story about preparing the ham, you, along with the mother and the granddaughter, can now decide what you believe and why you believe it. Each generation, in all things, can make their own decisions.

An uninvestigated belief system does no one any good, but those may be the beliefs we live by, and we may have no clue how to examine them. Often, those beliefs tend to become a form of religion. Challenging belief systems can be painful, and sometimes we avoid this challenge so we don't rock our internal boat. However, by going through the pain, you birth a new view and a newer you. It's like the real birthing experience a woman has with the birth of her child. You look at the fresh new beginning of life you hold in your arms, and you forget and forgive the pain. Pain turns to joy, but it is still needed to produce the new life. Both our physical bodies and our cerebral brains are always adjusting to forward growth. Think of how you looked first as a teenager, then in your twenties, your thirties, and on into the graying hair stage. Think of your thoughts as a toddler, teenager, and young adult, and whenever wisdom began to find you. Our views, perceptions, and beliefs will fit into our changing mental and physical modes. When we challenge our beliefs, we find fresh new growth for our current stage of life. When you look closely at belief systems (B.S.), do you get an "ah" feeling or do you flinch with a B.S. (bull sh**) feeling? Notice how you feel while staying with uncovering your thoughts.

Disenchantment may come with challenging belief systems. This disenchantment is a natural part of any significant transition which allows us to birth newness. At first, it can be difficult to see meaning in the disenchantment experience because disenchantment hurts. If you have ever broken up in a relationship, you may have experienced that disenchantment phase. In the early days of your relationship, there were many wonderful things to love about yourself and your significant other together. Then, you began to see that the relationship was not a perfect fit. Enchantment began to be traded for disenchantment. After the breakup, you felt sad and uncomfortable, but after a while, you began to feel whole and at peace again. If there wasn't any disenchantment beforehand, the breakup was probably a very painful process. Disenchantment helps us prepare for endings, as enchantment and disenchantment are both simply part of the natural rhythm of life. The process is similar in a job with which you have become disenchanted; your feelings helped propel you to search for another, better job. If you didn't feel disenchanted with the old job, you would not transition as easily and well into the new one. You would cling mentally to both the old job and the new one, which would make you feel torn and worn. Disenchantment helps one make a clean and clear decision.

We need to allow beliefs that no longer fit us that natural rhythm of disenchantment, too. As you poke at and turn your beliefs over to be studied, you are seeing what they hold for you. The thought of letting a disenchanted belief go can be scary. You may wonder what you can believe in after you let go of it. It's like asking, who will I fall in love with after the breakup? You will find your new belief and believe again, in time. But the outgrown belief must be cleaned away to make room for new possibilities. Like tilling and preparing a garden in the spring, this is work, but once cleared and prepared, you can plant seeds that suit your current needs. Newness grows, and in the summer and autumn, you will harvest your new thoughts and ways. Disenchantment can get you to wonderful newness.

In the enthusiasm of acquiring wonderful new beliefs, you may be tempted to push your own beliefs onto others, but it is important that you not do so. A sign of maturity is being at peace with your own beliefs without feeling the need to have others join you. You can have your thoughts or ways without needing to receive others' confirmation. How many people have tried convincing you that their political choice, religion, living style, or financial practices were the only ways to go? Did you appreciate it? Do you yourself do that to others? Can you hold your own belief without others' opinions influencing you or you trying to influence others? A sign of ultimate maturity is when you can be for something without being against something or someone else. This is holding onto what is yours without judgment.

Once you look at some of the beliefs in question, you can decide whether to keep them or toss them. You are the next generation to decide for yourself. You don't have to be held in any longer by the ideas of others. Don't let your beliefs take you somewhere you don't want to be only because others have gone there before you. Make your own values and ways! Forge your own path of beliefs. We all need to find our truths or beliefs. Everyone talks about finding "the truth" like it's a "one size fits all" thing out there somewhere. Our truths come from inside. They are a part of us because they are us. You are your beliefs and not the beliefs of others.

Stay alert, since you can revert back to old thoughts or false beliefs out of fear. Just ask yourself, does this feel comforting or agitating? Does it give you an "ah" feeling or a "B.S." feeling?

"Speak less and feel more."
—Renee Salvatori

Emotion

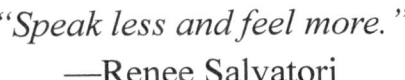

Where would we be without our emotions? Emotions add color to our lives. Have you ever seen the Skittles commercial on television showing the bright-colored candy pieces? The commercial encourages you to "taste the rainbow." Our own emotional commercial could be "feel the rainbow." Emotions are colorful expressions of us. Emotion is simply energy in motion (E-nergy/-Motion=emotion).

Emotions can be seen or unseen. Some emotions are vibrant while some are muted. A straight-faced person may not reveal the emotional energy of a sad person, just as a smiling person may not reveal the emotional energy of a truly happy person. Emotions may be surface readable or not, but our goal is not so much to see them as to feel them. How do you feel when you are happy, saddened, tender, loving, laughing, passionate, or distressed? Your emotions are your indicators. Emotional connection is not only the ability to recognize emotion but also to feel it.

Learning about emotions is an unconscious act. We casually mimic others' emotions starting at a very early age. We learn how to express, repress, resist, or deny them. Many are either running toward an emotion or away from one as we either accept or deny them. Emotional input allows us to hear our emotions' message, letting them guide and help us. Some people feel their emotions freely, and some keep their emotions so well hidden they themselves don't even acknowledge them. What about you? Do you give your emotions freely or keep them hidden? We need to feel them and not ignore them. Let them guide and help you. When we own our emotions, either by expressing them or quietly feeling them, our whole energy system remains healthy. When we suppress them, it distorts our physical and energy body, creating blocks. If we do not want blocks distorting us in any unhealthy manner, we need to find ways to express emotion.

When my son broke an ankle, he exhibited a physical emotion, but not the expected emotion; he walked on the broken ankle for two weeks and we never knew he was in pain. My other son twisted his ankle, and we knew about it early on. Both their responses and expressions of emotion to their physical pains were different, but each response was right for each boy. Emotion can also differ soulfully, as when two people watch a sad movie and one cries but the other doesn't. The one who has shed tears has been touched with emotion on a deep, soulful level; his friend has not been so touched. Our reactions to both physical and soulful feelings are emotions that are individual to each of us.

Sometimes emotions are not logical, though, so thinking through them doesn't help. You just need to experience and feel them. Some days you may need to put logic aside, and let emotions have the floor. Let them wash through you like a wave. You can let them go back out to sea if you don't want to contain them, but feel them first. There is a saying that breathing into an emotion is the opposite of taking a deep breath to escape it. Continue to go into and not away from your emotions. We are all humans with great emotion. We were not meant to be programmable robots. We are free-flowing living beings, flowing with emotional water. Feel into the humanness of you; recognize that your feelings are you. Cry for no reason if you need to. Laugh like a young carefree child. Don't act your age sometime. Ride the sled down the hill with your kids! Be serious if you want to be. If you feel tired or drowsy, lay around if you need to. Get angry if needed, but don't hurt anyone. Lose yourself in a song. Once, after listening to a song, my son said to me, "Mom, it gives me goose bumps and makes me feel happy." Now that is a perfect example of emotion and feeling.

Have you hidden your emotions behind thick walls? Try to let some of those walls melt down like a sun drenched snow fort. Those walls can be replaced with new spring blades of vibrant green grass that invite you into the vast meadow of colorful living. Emotions can be your ticket to a new spring season full of health.

When I stopped hiding in the shower or burying my face in my pillow to cry, I began to feel free to feel and be me. I was free to act on my feelings in each circumstance that came up, and I no longer stored my emotion to be vented at a later or more convenient time. When I held my feelings down for later, often my later time of convenience never came. I learned how to immediately roll with my emotion, which helped blend my mind and heart into one smoother movement, like rolling dough to incorporate all its ingredients. Teresa of Avila said, "The important thing is not to think much but to love much, so do that which best stirs you to love." Love is an emotion that stirs from the heart; it is not an emotion that comes from the head. Emotions speak from the heart, so don't let your head talk you out of them.

Some people are very dramatic emotionally, while others need a little prodding to release their emotion. Try not to judge people for having emotions, especially if they are not hurting you or others. What one person feels is a small thing might feel tragic to another. Men should have their emotions too, contrary to what society has suggested and reinforced. A crazy belief held by many is, you are not a man if you show any emotions. Please change that belief pattern immediately if you hold it! We should all have and express our emotions.

Emotions are more important than money in the bank, physicality, or relationships. They allow the full you to be present within.

If it has been awhile since you have felt your emotions, or if you have forgotten how to feel them, try to bring them out with music. Play a feel-good song, and notice how you feel. Switch to a sad song, and notice how you feel then. If you need a good cry, let the song help you. If you need a picker-upper, let the upbeat tunes give you a hand. Movies can work this way, too. The idea is to help you feel for your emotions again. Slowly, you will become more and more in touch with them. If we try to stuff emotions away or ignore them, we will do great harm to ourselves and possibly others. Let emotions flow the way they should and even be creative with them. You will realize that your emotions are constant, like weather that continually passes through. They are also like the tides that rise and fall. Just like weather and tides, your feelings are natural. They become E-Motion in motion. They are your color and your rainbow. They are your fluid body. They are your body's energy. Emotions are the touch-point to you, for they are you.

"A prayer in its simplest definition is merely a wish turned Godward."
—Phillip Brooks

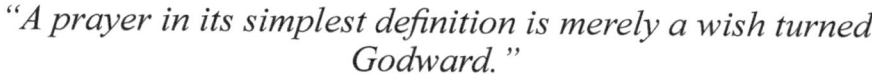

Prayer

Prayer is talking to God. It is a conversation, a petition, or an expression of gratitude. It is known as a powerful energy attractor. While prayer is our speaking, meditation is our listening. Some call this prayer, while others call it affirmations. How or where you pray or the words spoken do not matter. Our prayer or speaking can be said on our knees, with our hands in prayer pose, while bowing on the earth, when driving in the car, or when speaking as an open conversation. They can be silent, vocal, or written.

Prayer is both speaking from the heart and a birth from the heart. If we try to duplicate the prayers of priests or others, it is not our own genuine prayer because it doesn't come from our own heart. Have you ever listened to a small child's prayer? It is innocent because the words always come from his heart. My three-year-old once thanked God, after a boat excursion, by saying, "Thank you for letting the dolphins come out to play with me." It was so innocent and easy. Return to innocence and to your own simplicity.

Have you ever known what your child or partner was thinking even without their spoken words? God is like that too, only much better. God knows what is in our petitions or cries. Prayer isn't about words, but about God already knowing what we are trying to say. God is waiting for us to ask, just like a parent waits for his child to ask a special favor. Sometimes you don't offer help until your child petitions for your aid. In their asking, they are ready to receive.

Let go of any flashy ego as you speak to your Creator because posturing or flowing and grandiose words don't matter. There are no brownie points given out for what we say or how we say it. We are God's children, and our Creator is happy we are in each other's presence. Would you turn your own children away from speaking to you because they didn't speak in a grand fashion? To be in God's presence is all that truly matters.

If you absolutely do not know what to say or how to say it, just start by thanking God. Pretend you are at a Thanksgiving Day prayer celebration. Give thanks for something—anything you are thankful for. My next suggestion is to get a book of prayers. These will give you examples of how to start a phone line to God, Jesus, or whoever you call on. The prayers in the book shouldn't be duplicated, of course, but serve only as examples. Once, wanting to see what prayer was really all about, I read a prayer book, and after looking through it, I understood there was no set way to pray, and I could say whatever I liked. Prayer is your own personal conversation from your heart. I enjoyed, though, reading the poetry of others' words from their hearts. Your prayer can be a simple, "Roses are red, violets are blue, and God, I love you," or as lengthy as some of Robert Frost's poetic observations.

Some give up on prayer because they feel it does not work. They feel their prayers are never answered. I have to admit there was a time I felt the same. I prayed that my friend would be healed from cancer. Many prayers went up to God, and I begged and pleaded in tears. I did not understand that my prayer was selfish; it was coming from my desire to keep her with me. I realized I shouldn't have prayed for her healing as much as I should have prayed for her peace and comfort. I didn't want her to depart from this earth, but perhaps she was ready to go. It would have been better to pray for peace to surround her instead of for her healing.

It is hard to stay unattached to the outcome of our prayers, especially when our desire is great. Our requests can be like that Christmas list our children give us each year, very detailed and specific with great longing and expectation. When we put our trust in God and send up our petitions, we have to believe God will interpret our list and make the proper choices, just like we do for our own children. We may not get the desired color toy or the current model electronics, but God's gift will be exactly what we need. Prayers that are not granted are not necessarily unheard. Perhaps granting those prayers would not be beneficial to us, or perhaps our timing is not right. But learn to ask and talk anyway, no matter the outcome.

My favorite prayer or petition is that I have the highest and best outcome for the day ahead, and that only the highest and purest energy comes through. Some days, though, all I can manage are a few thank-you's. Other days the phone line stays open. Go ahead and whisper a prayer to God to converse, ask for help, or give thanks. The talk line is always open, and you don't need to go through anyone else to make your connection.

> *"Let us be silent that we may hear the whisper of God."*
> —Ralph Waldo Emerson

Meditation

Meditation is a space in our day to contemplate, center, hear God, or rest. This time allows the build-up of daily resistance to be released during a tiny part of the day, allowing the busy mind to get out of the way. Prayer is great because it causes us to focus by our words or thoughts. Meditating is taking in higher thoughts or just having quietness. It is that moment to come fully into you. Meditation is like the line from *The Wizard of Oz* when Dorothy says, "There's no place like home." Meditation feels like I am home.

Meditation is becoming increasingly popular in all walks of life because it has so many physical, psychological, and spiritual benefits and advantages. On a deeper level, with meditation we can align to a higher power and a higher self. We not only go deep within, but we also go higher. Our lives are filled with so much activity today, and we multitask continually. Our bodies are constantly moving, and our minds are constantly churning, even when we are still. Meditating is slowing down the body and mind and the control they can have on us at times. Remember the section on control and how micro-managing life is not beneficial? Well, sometimes our minds want to micro-manage us.

If you are a person whose mind is always full-steam ahead in twelve different directions, meditation is for you. Meditation will train you to focus on one thing at a time and to send all worry or annoyances into timeout.

In meditation, multi-tasking is not beneficial. It is like making love while your to-do-list is running through your head. Just as other thoughts are not welcome in your intimate love-making time, they are not welcome in your quiet meditative time. These are times when it is important to just let the moment be the moment.

I realized that most individuals, including myself, are good at asking, talking, and constantly moving. Many are not good at being still and listening. Perhaps this is why prayer is easy and meditation can prove difficult. We have to work harder at meditation and we should; its many benefits should not be shied away from.

We all need a little time without words or thoughts in our life. The practice of having both *internal* and *external* silence is imperative for well-being. It is in this silence that we find a new energy and true unity. There is much evidence that in quiet spaces, there is movement from head to heart. Knowledge is simply knowledge until it sinks into your heart. In the quiet, many new things can be realized and new understandings can be born. Our very being can germinate and grow into our truer selves. Have you ever felt that you wanted to be a more genuine person whose heart and head worked cohesively? Have you ever felt there were two of you living in one body? I longed to be in touch with my whole self, but I did not know how. I realized the more I meditated or just sat quietly, the more all parts of me merged together genuinely. Often, meditation brings greater understanding of our direction in life, too.

I know that in some parts of Italy, businesses close down for a couple hours every afternoon. When my husband spent some time there, he remarked how they have a different outlook to life and seem to be more relaxed; you have to wonder if it is in part because they get to relax and rejuvenate throughout their day. Some people go home and nap, and I liken their rest or napping to a meditation of sorts. Even lying down and resting is a chance for the mind to stop thinking. We here in the U.S. may not live in a country that honors downtime, but we can honor ourselves and find ways to give ourselves this mental rest, even if it is a nap that gets the mind and body to rest.

There are many ways to meditate, and I recommend that you find a way that feels comfortable to you. Find a comfortable position by sitting or lying down as you quiet your mind. You do not need to try to get anything from it. Just quietly be and try not to expect anything. You may immediately get the relaxation of it. You may get something like an intuition at that moment, later that day, or in a day or two. You will receive what you need, which may only be quiet. When you are quiet, you can even tell God or your higher self, "I am ready to hear anything you may like to tell me." It is your action of being still that shows you are sincere. Action often speaks louder than words.

My youthful religion frowned upon meditating. I had a huge mental block regarding meditation that took time to work through, and I struggled not to be afraid of it. I was taught meditation would open the mind to demons or other unwanted spirits. I know other religions teach this, so if you are like I was, I suggest investigating meditations that seem friendly and not scary.

No forbidden meditation on the self should ever be banned or discouraged. We should all come to know the divine light inside us. God belongs to all and is in all. Why continue to keep looking for God in different buildings and different lands when he is within you at all times? God is trying to come through, and meditating helps reconnect us to the source, or the main light bulb, in a sense. We do not have to be perfect for God to share wisdom with us; we only need a little solitude in which to hear Gods word. Lead a good life, follow your religion if you have one, but always place God first.

Carve out a small part of your day to meditate for this light.

Some people, even without religious upbringing that fears meditation, are scared to meditate for other reasons. They are genuinely afraid of silence. Thinking does have its place, but sometimes it's only a means to avoid ourselves. In silence, there are many truths heard. Don't run away, but try to spend a little time with yourself. You may actually begin to know you.

If you experience any of the discomforts mentioned, start slow and don't be too rigid about your practice of meditation. I had to start slowly. I found any way that I could get comfortable, and I took only the amount of time I felt safe with. Sometimes I could only handle three minutes, and other times my meditation resulted in sleep. If I couldn't tame my monkey mind, sleep would do it for me. Other times, my body would jerk me out of meditation because I just couldn't surrender to the silence. There were even times I would shake in fear or get panic attacks. Eventually, I stayed awake more and held quiet for longer periods of time. I felt like I was in training that would involve many starts and stops before it became my friend.

There are many ways to implement meditation or have a peaceful meditative state. What way you choose is up to you. Meditating casually is still one step closer than not meditating at all. One of the simplest meditations to begin with, though many do not think of it as meditation, is called "walking meditation" or "wakeful meditation." "Walking" or "wakeful" meditation is focusing on only the task at hand, without attaching other pending or perplexing issues. When you do dishes, just think of the dish in your hands and the warm soapy water. When you fold laundry, just feel the texture of the clothing and smell the clean aroma. When you take a walk, feel the ground beneath your feet and focus on the sensation of your feet rising and falling.

When you mow the lawn, be at peace with the moment and the smell of cut grass. If you are playing or making music, just enjoy the notes. If you are painting, get lost in creativity. Be as simple as you can be. You are not doing these tasks while thinking of a job outcome, your life, or your health. Just like meditative knitting or crocheting, you are enjoying the action to quiet the mind. You are not also watching television, listening to the radio, or carrying on a conversation in an attempt to multi-task. The challenge is to do nothing in the midst of doing.

The Taoist Chuang Tzu said, "If you cannot keep the mind still, that is called galloping while sitting." Try anything to get the mind to slow and stop thinking. Sit quietly and listen to soft music, letting the music calm you. Try to become the music. Try coloring with a box of colored pencils and let your mind just think of your picture and what color to use. Be slow and easy. Sit by water, whether ocean, creek, or fountain. Sit in water. Let the water carry your thoughts away. Repeat a mantra like AUM or OM; a religious name, like God or Buddha; a hum that feels soothing, or just the words *peace* or *calm*. You may want to focus on an image. Sit in nature under a tree or in the grass and contemplate nature. I have sat by a candle (even a battery candle) and focused on the flame until I began to feel calm. I have sat in a rocking chair (glider chair) and moved into calmness, like rocking a child to sleep. Find a place or a way to feel calm that is your own. I have used all these techniques to calm myself even before I went into a longer sitting meditation.

You don't need any formal training in meditation; everyone finds his own way, and each meditation will be different. Meditation is not sitting and going to La La Land like some imagine it to be, but instead, meditation is being centered and being present. Meditation is centering on the core spark in your very center when you quietly sit or lie down, close your eyes, and experience the slow and easy breathing of just being. In Buddhism, the highest discipline is self-observation without judgment while continually returning awareness to the centered breath. Have you ever just listened to your breathing in and out and thought it sounds like the ocean waves? I love the peaceful sound of the ocean waves rolling in and back out to sea. Like the Buddhist meditation, I am able to focus back to my breaths with the imagined ocean sounds. This peaceful "ocean thought" may help you, too.

There are meditative sitting positions, and there are also certain hand positions that many use. I don't use the hand positions, but you may at some point wish to search them out. When I sit, I soften my shoulders and tummy and picture myself looking like a little Buddha as I try to release any tension I am holding in my body.

A good suggestion for those new to meditation is to try to meditate in the same quiet location every day to encourage the development of a habit. Habits feel natural, which is helpful, especially if you are fighting any unease connected with meditation. Another suggestion is to have paper and pen with you in case your to-do lists start to circulate in your mind. Stop, open your eyes, and jot the list down for later. It may take ten stops, but eventually, you will not have to think about that to-do list when meditating. When the list is on paper, you can serenely proceed. Sometimes, random thoughts will make their way across your mind. That is okay. Let them float in and out. If we resist our thoughts, then an internal fight is waged. You can let them come in, say hello, and then leave. Eventually, you will find those random thoughts become less likely to pop up, even on crazy dramatic days.

Besides doing deep and slow breathing, you can use counting up or down stairs, elevator floors, or escalator levels to reach relaxation. Slow breathing or slow counting causes you to focus and gives you pause to calm. If techniques aren't working, try something new based on the knowledge you already have. One day, these simple counts and normal deep breaths just weren't working, so I mixed my routine. Instead of breathing in through the nose and out the mouth, I reversed and breathed in through the mouth and out through the nose. It was like rubbing my tummy and patting my head. I had to focus on this unnatural way of breathing. It worked because I was able to finally slow down and center myself. If you try this "backward" way, do have a glass of water beside you if possible because your mouth will get very dry! Have fun with your meditation practice. You, too, can get inventive.

The hardest part of meditation is learning to simply sit quietly and allow those minutes of inactivity. Do not feel guilty for giving yourself those minutes. Guilt will only sabotage your attempts. You are deserving of this quiet time. Allowing yourself this time can be the first and hardest challenge. The second challenge is getting the mind to be quiet. I recommend the breathing exercises, counting technique, or rocking/gliding yourself into calm before sitting meditation.

Caffeine or alcohol may not help your meditation efforts, as they can rev you up. Alcohol may calm at first but later it speeds up the heart. Sometimes having a light meal or snack made me feel comfortable enough not to fidget during sitting meditation, whereas a heavy meal made me feel uncomfortable. Turn off televisions, silence phones, and eliminate unnecessary distractions. When you meditate, don't try to "get" things from it, just relax and be content with the silence and yourself. Don't fight unavoidable sounds like a clock, a bark, or a car noise. Join them and become one with them. When you fight things, you struggle. When you surrender to the noise, you can be at peace with it as if it were part of your heart's rhythm.

The amount of time you do sitting meditation is your choice. If you can, allot time for calming first by breathing, counting, rocking, or whatever other technique you find helps. It is your meditation, so you get to determine its length, and any amount of time you give to yourself is of benefit. Some people start with five minutes and gradually lengthen their time. After the meditation is over, slowly refocus on your physical surroundings. Jumping quickly out of meditation's quiet is like an alarm's jolt to your system when you only wish to feel calmness. In fact, if you need to time your meditation, set a soft timer that will not startle you.

When I have trouble getting into meditation on my own, I use CDs to help. I have used musical CDs as well as CDs specifically geared toward meditation. They usually run about forty-five minutes to an hour, but of course, you only spend the amount of time you want to spend. A very good CD that continues to help me is *Getting into the Vortex Guided Meditations CD* by Jerry and Ester Hicks. Each fifteen minute track covers a different topic: General Well-Being, Physical Health, Relationships, and Financial Health.

You may be able to locate a meditation group in your area. The energy at these sessions is truly amazing. For me, in the sessions, it was as if I could float into mediation on someone else's coat tails, so to speak. The centering energy can be so collective in these gatherings. Some of my better meditations have been this way. I seem to get very visual mind pictures and very clear thoughts. There also is a very peaceful feeling as everyone in the room is also reaching for that peaceful state.

There is a saying, "Do you walk the dog or does the dog walk you?" which is like the saying, "Do you walk your mind or does your mind walk you?" As I mentioned, meditating does not come easy to me. One night, as I asked celestial heavens for help in my meditation endeavor, I got a quick vision of a woman and her little puppy. This was the same woman and puppy I saw five days a week walking to get her children from school. I saw them as I waited to pick up my own children. The puppy was a rowdy little thing at the beginning of the school year; it would pull on the leash, or sit down and refuse to move. As the months moved forward, I marveled at how much better the puppy became at walking in synch with the woman. Then I had my meditation vision. This little puppy was grown, graceful, and beautifully strolling along to its destination. There was no fight, just ease. The puppy represented me and what could happen if I kept training my mind. I decided to keep working with meditation in the hope that someday I, too, will just stroll along into my higher self. It pays to keep "walking your dog."

More often than not, I work hard at my meditation; very rarely can I just roll easily into it. Again, in one of those difficult moments, I just couldn't push the pause button on my mind. (Sometimes, I literally picture me pushing the pause button so I can meditate, but the image wasn't working that morning.) So I thought of the Harry Potter movie, *Deathly Hallows Part II*, when Harry was between life and death. He walked into a brightly lit room where Dumbledore, once the wise headmaster, sat. Harry quietly waited until Dumbledore spoke to him. I thought what if I like Harry Potter, could just leave my activities and walk into God's presence? I could be with my own wise headmaster…which is what meditation ultimately leads to. So I pictured myself walking into this brightly lit room and sitting quietly. That visual has worked for me many times. I have also pictured myself outside as a tree with my feet growing roots, and as I become grounded, my branches and leaves reach towards the sky to peace and calm. As I exhale, my leaves and flowers are forced to unfold. As I inhale, my roots push further into the earth. Many people have success with this meditation image; it was one of my own first successful endeavors, and I go back to it often.

Have you seen the new washing machines? You push the start button and the machine latches so the lid can't be opened while the machine runs. Maybe our meditations can be like those new machines. Once we start, the lid of our mind latches so we can finish the cycle without interruptions. When the latch releases, we are clean and fresh.

Do not get discouraged as meditation is not easy. Many have had difficulty in the early stages. The practice of learning meditation is a practice, and it will take time. The only way to rise above thought is to stop constant thinking, which may seem unnatural and stressful to you at first, but the wonderful thing about meditating is, it increases your ability to handle stress. Make meditation a priority as it is probably one of the most important things you can do to increase your enlightenment and health. Decreasing your stress level is also an added benefit.

May you be blessed with the stamina to keep trying so you reach the blessings of meditation's benefits! Again, as the wise masters say, "The journey of incredible discovery is the distance traveled from our head to our heart." The path of healing is in the finding of oneself. Turn off a piece of the day, and hug your soul.

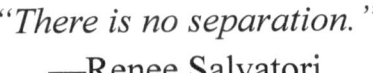

"There is no separation."
—Renee Salvatori

God or Creator

There are many names for our creator: God, Goddess, Supreme Being, Alpha and Omega, Heavenly Father, Heavenly Mother, Creator, Creative Force of Universe, Jehovah, Yahweh, Allah, Jesus, Muhammad, Light of All Lights, Divine One, Divine Light, Source, Essence of Life, Zoroaster, Buddha, Adonai, Elohim, Lord, Inner Being, and many more. The name you or your religion chooses to use truly does not matter. Like the saying, "I don't care what you call me, just don't call me late for dinner," God might say, "I don't care what you call me, just call me."

If you think of how a child addresses a mother, he may use words like *momma, mother, mommy, mom*, or *mum*. All these words have the same meaning. A grandfather can be referred to as *grandpa, grandfather, poppy, pap pap*, or *gramps*, and again, all forms of the endearment refer to the same person. Humans, from every corner of earth, need to stop judging what others call their maker.

Have you noticed that Eastern and Western Gods can be invented and defined differently? Even in different sections of the same country, our Gods can be described differently. Some see their God as vengeful, exacting, and dark. Some see their God as loving, forgiving, and fun. God truly wants to be close to you and to be in your presence. All we have to do is open our hearts to God; God does not need to be found or worshipped in a church, temple, or synagogue. God is a piece of every one of us and is in all of us. Try to picture a foam cup which is poked full of tiny holes, and then hold that cup up to a light source like a lightbulb. The light will shine out of all those tiny holes. God is the bulb and we are the light shining through. Our light never goes out and never diminishes because we are a piece of the Source. Since God is eternal, his light is eternal. Only we ourselves can diminish this Source by disallowing the light to come to us and through us. By diminishing this light, we make our God judgmental and angry and even nonexistent. God is with us everywhere we go, if we allow. God is like sunshine warming our faces or like love emanating from our insides, again, if we allow. Let others have their own endearing name, label, or description of the Creator with no more playground or battleground fights of, "My God is better than your God." God is one and the same and is everyone's main light bulb or light source. We need tolerance in allowing others to have and hold their own opinions of this light.

Not everyone believes in God or finds God endearing. Some are mad at God because of their life experiences. What happens when we get mad? We strike out somewhere and sometimes we strike out at God because God created us and our woes. Some are mad God hasn't made a better world, better people, or better circumstances for those people. When we get mad and wounded, walls go up and we barricade ourselves from the Source.

Some of us have heard very contradictory stories about God. These stories may have originated in childhood and followed us into adulthood and the present time. Some stories paint a very judgmental and mean God. One minute God loves you, and the next, God is judging you. After so many years of negative stories and possibly bad things happening to you, you refuse to investigate the other side. Like the gossip about a person that goes around town, work, or school, these stories might make you hesitate about even meeting this person let alone thinking differently about him because you have drawn pictures in your mind or jumped to conclusions based on those stories you heard. Sometime later, you may get to know this person, and then you begin to understand that the stories were false or based on someone else's personal belief. You may even wonder how you could have misjudged. How have years of stories about God painted your picture? Feel with your heart and not your head and see where that leads you.

God is never mean or judgmental, as some scriptures say. God does not hold a grudge, nor does God want us to, either. God does not exact inequities from one generation to another or for generations upon generations. He will never tell us to blow up a plane or buildings, beat our spouses, or go to war with the slogan, "God bless our country more than yours." Yes, war may be necessary at times to protect us, like locks on our homes are necessary, but God does not bless one country or house over another country or house. God is in us all, even when and while our ego is working negatively to make us think we are better than someone else. When ego is taken out of God, God becomes pure energy, pure love, pure grace, and pure forgiveness. God, like a loving parent, will never guide his children to pain. God is a creator of all good. Throughout millennia, we have let our egos lead us rather than the true God. We need to feel with our own hearts for the true story of God. Let's try to change future history, at least for ourselves.

We all explain our God from our own perceptions and perspectives. We interpret God from our own thoughts and feelings. I have made my God masculine because that is what felt comfortable to me. I have a friend who needs the feminine, and she envisions her God with a soft touch and a soothing voice. My friend, I, and other religions see the same God in different ways and by different names. However, there is only one God. We are all connected to Him, but we allow ourselves to be disconnected by diversity. We invent our own agreements and disagreements over what God says or wants. We can easily make ourselves believe God wants something different on the other side of the world; once we believe that, it is easy to believe God wants something different on the other side of a room, and then on the other side of our minds. We are all extensions of Pure Energy, and when we are loving, joyful, and clear minded, we are truly one with the Divine Source.

Let there be no more crusades against others in the name of God or religion. When we fight or dispute with others over their faith or for the God they worship, we devalue their beliefs. We were made to be diverse, and instead of wasting time thinking everyone's God or beliefs should be the same as your own, learn to appreciate others the way they are! Like Robert Fulghum said about crayons, "We could learn a lot from crayons; some are sharp, some are pretty, some are dull, while others bright, some have weird names, but they all have learned to live together in the same box." When you are painting, would you rather your canvas be a single color or a multitude of colors? Isn't the painting with an assortment of colors more interesting? It's the same thing in life. When you have diversity around you, your life is more interesting. Helen Keller said, "Face your differences and acknowledge them; but do not let them master you, let them teach you patience, sweetness, and insight." If you have ever thought of reincarnation in a positive, probable light, we have probably all been Christian, Muslim, Jewish, Hindu, Buddhist, atheist, and agnostic at one time or another. Throughout our lifetimes, we have all probably been sidetracked by ego and confusion. We all understand better today that no matter what we call our God or our religious preference, we are all seeking connection to the main light bulb or pure source. We can learn tolerance, which includes acceptance for those who don't have tolerance towards us.

We are all moving along *our own paths*. That's all it is, nothing less and nothing more. If you find your path in a church, at home, in nature, while meditating, with God, or anywhere else, *all is well*. God blesses you all, so call on who you need, whether it is Allah, God, Jehovah, Muhammad, Light of All Lights, or whatever other name you use for the Creator. God is not separate from any of us, but He will never force Himself on anyone who does not want the Light. If you are ready, you can feel the full warmth of God's light and love because it is for and in each of us. It is a pulsed energy in our hearts. God's presence is in every living thing. God shared your mother's womb with you and gave you your first breath. God is in the grandbaby you cuddle and that meal that nourishes your body. God is in that beautiful vacation spot, and God is in the sound of a calm rain. God is our friend and not our foe. One day, may you allow God's love to shine on your face as well as from your heart.

*"I have no objections to churches
so long as they
do not interfere with God's work."*
—Brooks Atkinson

Religion and Church

Religion is an organized approach to God. Some people need this approach, and some do not. Some also need the community that a church or a religion holds for them. A place of worship to some is not so much an obligation as a commune with people of like minds. To some, it is a normalcy in their lives and those scheduled services and events are eagerly awaited. Religion may also be a place they feel an energy that rejuvenates their soul and helps them go another day or week. Some may get this same feeling with a support group, a meditation group, a book club, or a golf or tennis group. Get the idea? So if it is religion or a place of worship that you need, don't feel guilty and don't feel judgmental of those who don't need it. Do understand, my friends, that formal religion is not needed to find God or to become enlightened or awake. Enlightenment transcends religion. Spirit and spirituality are not a religion.

To some, a church, a temple, or a synagogue is a sacred place. They feel a vibration upon entering the building that resonates within them; they are uplifted even if only standing in its silence. Have you ever simply stood in a place and felt an energy that was great or comforting? There are sacred places other than religious houses that many overlook; you may have your own personal sanctuary right in your own home or you may have a sacred spot outside in nature. Some of these uncommon places can also be termed a church.

Don't feel limited to religion or church, as there are so many other ways a person can find their connection to God. John Wesley said, "The Bible knows nothing of any one solitary religion," and the scripture of 1 Corinthians 3:16 adds, "Do you not know that you are the temple of God and that the Spirit of God dwells in you?" Some may find their religion or church within themselves. I remember hearing someone say, "My religion is kindness." What or where is your religion or house of worship?

Religion and places of worship are like a support group to some. Sometimes you find a good one and sometimes you don't. I also say that church and psychologists' offices cannot be "forced" or "guilted" on anyone. If a person does not want to be in that place, he will only be there in body. My husband goes to church every week, as that is how he feels connected and grounded in his faith; he even seeks out churches on vacation. The first thing I do when I get into a new town is look for food markets and restaurants. We share the same phonebook but look under different sections. He and I never berate each other over this difference. His soul is filled up in his way, and it makes him beautiful to me.

Religion and a place of worship can make your life easier because it can support you in finding God. However, take heed: Religion can also take you off your course in finding God and yourself. Sometimes, we call upon God through religion as if God is separate from us, but God is in all of us at every moment.

When we compare the Old and New Testaments of the Bible, it feels like two separate Gods are depicted. The Old Testament, Genesis through Malachi, gives a picture of an angry and wrathful God who needs anger management classes. When we read the New Testament, Matthew through Revelations, we see a God who finds happiness based on what others do. It looks like God cannot find inner happiness that is unconditional. God can, but we are not taught that. Don't let religion pull you off your course to who you are or who you are becoming because spirituality and religion are two different things.

Many spiritual beings, throughout the millennia, have come before humanity to help us live better lives, but I will write of Jesus since he is the spiritual figure with whom I am most familiar. While I love Jesus and find his life very inspirational as a role model of walking a perfect path, I truly don't feel God is only giving us one spiritual leader or spiritual avenue in life. The road in life may be short, but it is also wide. How can we go wide when we narrow our vision to only one spiritual being (whether inspired or not)? How can we go deep when we are encouraged to go through someone else? We find so many discrepancies that we no longer hold the Bible as the only way to get us to our heaven and/or inner peace. Yes, there is much good advice in the Bible, but there are many conflicting pieces of advice, too. The Bible has served and serves its purpose and still does for some, but other ways of becoming one with God are evolving.

More and more people cannot buy into the Bible being divinely inspired any more than our own divinely inspired selves. Yes, the Bible is as inspired as the book I am writing is inspired, just as the children's book you read to your child last night was inspired. Many people genuinely love the Bible, and many study it extensively and live their lives devoted to it. Some spend their lives explaining the Bible in churches, communities, and other countries. There is nothing wrong with this. I hesitate only briefly in saying this, but I feel the Bible is becoming more and more just an amazing inspirational book on morals, history, and pearls of wisdom. The book's binding is no longer holding us in, just as we no longer cling to the hem on our mother's skirt. We are unraveling years of stitches. We are cutting ourselves free of threats, negativity, and judgment, whether coming from the God of the Bible or people and situations in our lives. People are looking for inspiration without judgment from beings like Zen Masters, Confucius, Jesus, the Dalai Lama, the Buddha, Saints, Mother Mary, Mother Teresa, other inspired beings, and even themselves. They are starting to feel and see a truly loving God in a different way. Do not let religion or the God of old pull you off your path.

Again, please remember that spirit or spirituality is not a religion. I was raised in a religion that required us to go to church three times a week. We were encouraged as children not to belong to any extracurricular sports or hobbies that needed participation on those nights or days. We were encouraged not to have jobs that interfered with those church times. We were also encouraged to do community outreach work several hours per month, on top of the other times reserved for church activities. Do you know how hard it was as a kid to participate in any school functions or get a job that didn't include those particular days and times?

I remember one time watching grown men from the congregation making plans to go see a live football game one Sunday instead of going to church.

I heard the chatter of the church's people judging how wrong this excursion was. They felt those men and everyone else who did not go to church at the appointed times were not only wrong but were also bad influences on others. God is not judgmental like some people think. If you want that much church in your life and it feels good for you, then have it, but keep your desires centered on yourself. God wants us to enjoy the physical part of our time on this planet as much as our spiritual enlightenment. Do you really think God sits around and judges men for going to a football game, teenagers for joining band or basketball teams, or anyone for holding down a job on a Tuesday night? Some of our best enlightenment lessons are when we integrate with those around us who are not of our own faith. We learn patience and insight by integrating with diversity. We learn tolerance in the biggest sense. We also learn our own truths when we live life to the fullest, which involves integrating both spiritual and physical. We are here to experience physical realities: nature, music, creative endeavors, socializing, family, friends, and church if it feels good to you, but remember, enlightenment transcends religion and any church.

Go the path that resonates with you. Your path is always changing as are the sources you choose from. If it is a house of worship or a religion that gives you the comfort food you are looking for, then by all means partake of it! May you also be blessed with the best quality people with whom to commune in all areas of your life.

*"Leave room in your heart
for angels to dance."*
—Anonymous

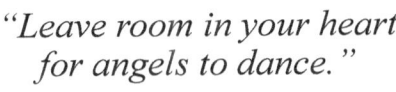

Angels

Angels! This has got to be my favorite subject on which to write. I just love them so much! For ages, humans have fought over God, but very few people seem to fight over angels. I do consider many people on earth to be what we call earth angels, but I am going to speak about angels of the celestial kind. Like God, they are referred to by many names: Archangels, Seraphim, Al Malaikah, Malakh, Guardian Protector, Divas, and many others of which I am unaware. Angels do not belong to any religious sect. They are nondenominational. You do not need to change your views or beliefs to work with them. They do not want to be worshipped. That is saved for the Light of All Lights, Power of All Powers, God, or whatever name you use for the Creator. My mother takes her requests only to God, even though she believes in angels. Even if you believe in God, you can also work with and have a relationship with angels. In Psalms 91:11 it says, "For He shall give His angels charge over you, to keep you in all your ways." God not only gives us permission to have these relationships, but he lovingly has provided angels in our lives. I love talking to the angels and feeling their support in so many ways.

We all have many angels with us right now. We each have Guardian Angels who have been with us from the moment we were born and will stay with us until our physical death. We are all born with at least one

Guardian Angel. How much love and excitement God must have felt giving these wonderful beings to help and support us in our life! I bet you have given a welcoming baby gift to a newborn child. It was probably given with excitement and much love. Can you imagine God giving us our Guardian Angel in much the same way? Not only has God given us Guardian Angels but has also given many other angels for our support. God is a great gift-giver.

Angels are messengers directly from God who give us guidance. They are pure beings of Divine Light who are trustworthy and want to help us in all areas of our lives. The word *angel* means "messenger of God." How fun and special to have our own postal carrier! We all have snail mail, email, knee mail, and wing mail. How fast is wing mail? Very! Angels will quickly carry messages between Creator and created.

Many people feel that deceased loved ones are their angels, but this is not the case. Loved ones who have passed away fall into the category of spirit guides. Spirit guides can act like angels because they can be very wise and loving, but their guidance isn't as pure. Spirit guides have free will and have been in human form at one time, while angels do not have free will and have never had a human body. Our spirit guides are always ready to assist us, just like our guardian angels. Like our guardian angels, we all will have at least one spirit guide in life. But unlike our guardian angel that stays with us from our birth to our death, spirit guides come and go according to our particular needs.

You can ask for more angels because there are an infinite number available to everyone. There are benefits to being surrounded by additional angels. Work with them as a team. Talk with them, either verbally or mentally. If writing out your thoughts is easier, write to them. A sentence or two, a note, or a full letter—whatever you write may untangle what you're holding in your head and heart. I have done all of these, depending on what I needed at the time. Remember, what you say or write, or even how you say or write, is unimportant.

You can ask for help or just have a conversation with your angels as your friends or team members. Don't forget to thank them for being with you and helping you.

We all have free will, and our angels (like God) will never interfere if you are not interested. They want to be a part of your life, but you have to ask. There is nothing too big or too small for them to help with. Don't think you are keeping angels from more important things, as they have unlimited time and energy; there is nothing more important than helping you. Don't sabotage yourself into thinking you are not worthy enough. I have learned through my own healing that we are all worthy, but we may not be willing. If you feel there are many things wrong in your life that is truly when and why you need your angels most. They love you unconditionally.

You can ask their help for so many things. You can ask them to surround and be with you, your loved ones, or a situation. They can help with all kinds of relationships, including relationships with partners, children, friends, neighbors, or work associates. They can help you find shelter or a home. People have been helped in finding jobs or lost items. Ask for angelic protection wherever you are. I ask them to be stationed at the corners, windows, and doors of my home and to be with me while I am driving. They can help you release emotional toxins and clear out old issues with people living or deceased. Ask them to help you fulfill your life's purpose. Their help is always there as you go through changes in your life. They await your call.

They act on your call immediately, whether you sense them or not. If you call on them, they are there. If you feel your angels are not helping you, it may be because you do not feel worthy of their help. *You are worthy; you are worthy; you are worthy!* Please, understand that. You don't ever have to do something to earn your worthiness. You are born worthy. Not being able to hear their answer could also be from not wanting to hear it because it is not the answer you hoped for. How much of their guidance do you trust?

Some prayers, through perfect timing, are answered immediately, while other prayers will need time before being answered. In hearing answers, you need to stay open and patient. Honor thoughts or feelings that come to you, especially if they are repeated. Messages you receive will be very simple, but if they seem unclear, ask for clarity. Divine guidance repeats itself, while false guidance or your own ego's answer will usually and eventually fade away when ignored. Angels' characteristics are love and light—always. Love and light cannot be faked. If you hear things that are not from love and light, do not listen or respond. You do not need to work hard at the hearing part. Be *easy*. Let them do the work instead of you chasing after their voices. It is hard to chase anything when you do not know the direction from which it is coming. Angels know where you are and can direct their help with pinpoint precision. Try to breath, close your eyes, and quiet your environment. Try getting into nature for those trying times when you really need their support.

I have read that messages are carried on molecules of oxygen. So, the more fresh air we get, the louder their messages. Go outside in nature or near water, then listen and feel.

If you would like to hear from your angels more often, talk with them more often. Try practicing by asking them a question, then listen to see if any of the four ways listed below give you an answer. You will learn to distinguish between their help and your ego. Just as in our dreams, you know beyond a doubt the difference between a dream that has significance and one that was just your brain downloading data from a busy day. Our dream state can sometimes be just like a parrot downloading all the words from the day right before it goes to sleep. Our dream can be a jumbled download holding no significance, or it can be a dream of importance. If you haven't already, you will learn to distinguish a parrot-type download from an important message.

Here are some ways angels can be with you:

1) Physically or emotionally with a gut feeling, a tingling, a hunch, goose bumps, or just an awareness they are with you.

2) Visions and dreams while you are awake or asleep. You may see them in body form or as flashing lights.

3) You may have knowingness, when you just know wisdom that exceeds your own.

4) You may hear words or sounds outside your ears.

5) You may hear your name or others' names. You could hear a song that holds a meaning or hear a piece of a conversation that seems just for you.

Angels do have characteristics that give them male or female energies, and they have been known to take brief physical forms, but this does not make them spirit guides as they only do this in times of crisis or extreme stress. Angels are usually translucent and semi-opaque, and they glow in different colors according to their energy. Their clothing looks opalescent. Artists who originally painted them mistook their glowing auras for halos and wings and portrayed them this way. Some artists portrayed the auras as large wings, but these wings are not used to fly. After years of seeing winged and haloed angel portraits, we expect angels to have wings and halos, and if that is what our minds expect, then angels will accommodate us with a winged appearance. You can also see angels as flashing or colorful lights. Angels will appear in whatever guise you will recognize them in. It is also normal if you never see these auras, wings, or lights. You may just have a feeling or know they are in your life.

Like God, the angels love you more than you know, and this love is unconditional. Angels overlook our idiosyncrasies, personalities, and egos to focus on the Light and Love in each of us. We can focus on their love, too. They are open 24/7 around the clock and around the globe. Just ask! Angels truly are here waiting to give us their support, love, and confidence. Make a new friend today. Years ago Garth Brooks wrote a song, "I've Got Friends in Low Places." I've changed the words and now sing my own song, "I've Got Friends in High Places." I remember the day worry was lifted from me like magic. I realized I didn't have to feel like I was going through life on my own. Imagine the freedom and release when you can look up and say, "Help! I don't want to do this alone anymore!" Angels are God's gifts to us, but we have to decide to open and use this gift.

I will share an angel story of my own. While I was writing this book, I grew more and more doubtful, and I played all the "what ifs" and "I don't knows" over and over again in my head. I wanted more peace internally than I was allowing myself. I lay in bed one night overwhelmed with growing uncertainty, so I randomly pulled two cards from my *Angel Oracle* card deck by Doreen Virtue, and as I read them, I was reassured.

The first card said something in the regard that Archangel Michael was working with me to help me release old fears and reach new heights of happiness and peace. Wait, it gets even better! The second card said something like detach from the surrounding emotions and Archangel

Michael will help by cutting with his flaming sword any attachment to fear or drama so I could be centered in peace. It suggested I became embroiled in a situation to the point that I could not see it objectively. It advised that I step back to access a sense of inner peace which will lead to new and helpful insights. Boom! There it was! Out of all the cards in the deck, those were the two I picked. I was supported by angels, as we all are when we ask.

Sometimes, we can't change our vision to see that angels really are here. When we are stressed, science shows us our peripheral vision narrows so we are unable to focus on other things and we are left with tunnel vision. Sound familiar? It is part of the flight or fight syndrome of bygone days when we ran from wild animals, and it is still very active and alive today. The wild animals have changed, though. When we are running from a tiger, we do not need peripheral vision. The only vision we need is straight ahead vision to get us to safety. That night, my hyper-stressed mind was not allowing me to relax enough to let my vision soften. So, I pulled those two cards, hoping for insight, and I received my answer.

For fun, here is a letter I wrote to my guardian angel. I share these personal thoughts with you, not only to make you smile, but to perhaps encourage you to talk or write to your own Guardian Angel. Have fun with your angel friends!

Dear Guardian Angel,

Thank you for all that you have done and do for me. I am sure I have given you a celestial heart attack, mystified you with my dumbness, or had you shaking your halo in contemplation at me. I am sorry. I know you don't expect any apologies from this earthling in your care, but I feel I would like to give you one anyway to ease my own conscious. On the other hand, I hope I have made you proud, and I hope to have given you a good laugh every now and again.

I think I know you from my dream back in 2002. I thank you for your expression of kindness that night. When I light my angel nightlight by the desk, I think of you and perhaps any other angels I or my family may have. I think of Archangel Michael and all the many others we have. I believe in you, and I also love you!

Open Your Heart to the True You

Thank you for being with me and taking care of me. You have done a wonderful job. May we have many more wonderful years together? You are my friend with wings.

In Love and Appreciation,
—Renee

> *"Even a volcano can finally release its
> inner contents to experience calmness."*
> —Renee Salvatori

Anger and Release

When anger is felt, a powerful force or vibration makes its presence known in many ways. Anger is not a bad thing; it is only an emotion. No one should tell you not to be angry, as that is denying you an emotion or release you may need. Remember, even Jesus was filled with indignation and overturned the tax collectors' tables in the temple! Some people ignore feelings of anger, jealousy, and hatred because churches tell you God has labeled them as sins. These people suggest we go straight to forgiving, but ignoring anger is not a positive action. When you ignore or take a different way around anger, you do what counselors call a "spiritual by-pass," which stresses your body's systems (especially the heart) and could lead to a real heart by-pass later. Go through anger and not around it if you want to get to the end of it.

Think of yourself driving; your choices are to go straight through the city or to drive around the city's outer border. Going through the city will be quicker but will have more traffic, whereas the country route will be more scenic and have less traffic but will take you longer. When you decide not to deal with anger, you are taking the scenic journey around the issue. You can do some sightseeing and take your time, but your path around your anger will have time to become bigger and more embellished. Going through issues may not be the easiest way, but it will be the quickest way. We need to acknowledge that we are angry or upset and have our emotion before finding a way to safely extinguish it.

Open Your Heart to the True You

There are two kinds of people, those who are aware of their anger and those who are in denial about it. There are also two kinds of anger, one that exhibits classic volcano signs (red face, vocalizations, crying, kicking, or throwing) and one camouflaged behind a smiling face. This "sweet anger" is a slow and steady interior burn that may be even worse than exploding like a volcano and getting the anger out. (Just don't hurt anyone in getting anger out because then you may have guilt issues to work through later.) Also, if you don't get anger out over the issue that is the real culprit, you may constantly be angry over insignificant things that really aren't the problem. Don't be fooled; anger is anger, and whether volcanic or sweet will wreak havoc on you.

Holding onto anger or grudges by stalling or refusing to go through the pain of confrontation makes you suffer needlessly. This bitterness creates stress in us in many ways and can become a silent killer, so it is beneficial to release your anger as quickly as you can. If we live with anger day after day, it's like you're recycling it. The anger will keep resurfacing until you deal with it. Start to become aware of anger you want to release. As Ralph Waldo Emerson said, "We are not free to use today or to promise tomorrow because we are already mortgaged to yesterday." Are you holding onto yesterday's anger? There are two things we cannot change: other people and the past. The past is the past! Hanging onto resentment is like letting someone you don't like live rent free in your head. When we work through anger and resentment, we free up our energies to live today. Release what you no longer need. Pay off your mortgage and move into the future…debt free.

We have labeled people or situations in our minds as "unforgivable," and we create a lot of tension for ourselves by defining them as such. When we keep making others and ourselves pay dearly for wrongs, we are in a state of unrest. Do we double-indemnity over and over? Would we want others to do that to us? Forgiving and letting go of anger towards a situation or a person does not mean you have to like the situation or the person. You can if you want to, but you don't have to. Sometimes, we can fall into the arms of someone, perhaps a lover or a parent, after they have wronged us and know beyond a doubt they are so very sorry. If those arms can become your fortress, then yes, by all means love them. Other times, this is not so easy. I am sure Jesus forgave the soldiers and Pontius Pilate who orchestrated and carried out his death. However, his experience before and surrounding his death was intense, and he would not have wanted to keep reliving that time over and over again, so he forgave and moved on. Sometimes the hurts and anger we experience are a ways to a means, like Jesus' was, and learning to like the individuals or situations involved is not obligatory.

What has anger or suffering meant to you? Has it taught you to move with and through emotion, to learn forgiveness, compassion, sympathy, and humanity? Think of the analogy of the white horse with the rider dressed all in white verses the black horse with the rider dressed all in black. One symbolizes good, while the other symbolizes bad. However, sometimes the black horse, or the big irritant, can offer us the biggest growth opportunity. Who knows why we sometimes meet up with that black rider and who truly is the good or bad guy?

When we forgive, it does not mean we wish to have the person who wronged us be a friend of ours or sleep under our roof. To forgive means you release the attachment you held, which was bitterness. You may never know why you had or have to suffer, but if you can get past that internal suffering, you can have the future free. Clouds of resentment and anger only keep you from seeing the sun. Jesus, and all other victims of injustices who have found the light of forgiveness, pushed that dark cloud of anger away and no longer held the lasso around it. It is not easy to forgive, but when your health and mind can't bear the stress any longer, you will know beyond a doubt it is time to be free.

Understand that forgiveness can come in waves over the same issue; you may not forgive all at once. I had an issue in which I truly felt I had forgiven a certain person. I forgave and felt many tears that washed away the anger and pain. More than five years later, a memory blindsided me over the same issue and took me into another level of forgiveness. The first time I forgave, I forgave angrily through stubborn tears, feeling like a victim. The second time, it was from a much deeper place; the memory was so intense I felt I couldn't breathe as I cried from the deepest part of my soul. With that second round of forgiveness, I realized I had forgiven on yet another, much deeper level. I liken forgiveness to the onion skin analogy. Sometimes with initial forgiveness, we merely peel back the first layer. Sometimes, to truly forgive, we have to peel back more layers and go deeper. As we uncover deeper levels, the smell or the pain will be stronger. Whether your forgiveness is an easy one or a more difficult one will depend on yourself and the pain you feel.

Forgiveness is from your own soul and not something pacified by other actions. Here is what I mean. My son and I were discussing how he could let go of a grudge he held over his brother hitting him. One day, my son announced he was over his grudge because in a game of Nerf Target, a friend shot his brother and my son felt that was retribution enough to let his previous injury go. He felt his brother's hurt evened the score. Enjoying and celebrating the fact that the person who "did you wrong" got his just reward, even from another person, is really not forgiving the grudge or anger. The grudge is still alive and active and only being temporarily released by the other's misfortune. Feeling relief by witnessing another's trouble or getting revenge through a hit man, so to speak, is not resolving anger.

Here are some ways to safely release anger and deep pain. Some release techniques are easy ones, like telling our children they may hit a couch or a bed, but not their siblings. This sort of substitution can give an immediate release, even to adults. Walk outside and do some deep breathing. Yell into the woods or throw rocks into a river. What about when hitting that mattress has no soothing effect because the anger is too deep? Try writing it out. Write from the deepest and most despairing places of your heart or soul. Let the pain and thoughts go out of those despairing places, through your hand, and finally onto the paper. Cry or yell if you need to. When you are done, go outside and burn it. Let the misery burn away and be destroyed. The ashes will release the held in burden of pain.

Another way to release even a long held in anger is called the "anger safe bubble," Physically take your arms and draw an imaginary bubble around yourself. Inside the bubble, place figures to whom you feel connected, like Jesus, your guardian angel, the archangels, or God. While you and your support team are in this safe bubble, state what anger or unforgiveness you would like to release. You may feel the urge to cry, scream, write, punch the air or a bag, do karate kicks (make sure you are well grounded so you do not hurt yourself), or some other physical action. After you are finished moving, make the bubble smaller. Collapse and condense it until it fits in your hand. Now hand it over to Jesus, the archangels, God, or whoever you placed in the bubble earlier. Ask them to take it and dispose of it by perhaps dropping it into a volcano for complete destruction. Is the anger gone? Is part of it gone?

Keep working at any of these suggestions. You may try a few times before all the imbedded parts of your anger have emerged, depending on how deep the pain or how long you have held onto it. Your anger is coming from the inside out, and sometimes that inside is a very deep place. You may have to remove a lot of rubble to find the clear, flowing river inside yourself.

Sometimes childhood memories hurt the most because in childhood we were so tender and trusting. Our hurts could be from many things—a parent who just didn't know how to parent, teachers who may have maimed us needlessly, nicknames, sibling rivalries, school mates bullying or belittling, sexual abuse, verbal or physical abuse, our own hurts we did to ourselves. These hurts can be carried over into our adult years and run very deep. Being an adult does not mean childhood hurts will disappear with age. They may still need an outlet.

When you give yourself over to healing, you may find one memory leads to another memory. Bad memories don't go away simply because we are aware of them or because we have buried them with age. Isn't it time to face them and begin healing? Once we start to work through bad memories, they will eventually lose the power they once had, and it will feel good to release those bad boys. Picture your hurts written in sand that dissolve with the waves of the sea. Sometimes therapy or support groups can greatly aide in the process. You always have your God and angels for support in this endeavor. Just remember to ask.

What if a long withheld anger is not over someone else, but over you? That personal anger can be released too. Anger and guilt can stem from something big that happened in your life or from something very small, like feeling you've been a bad parent for a day. Try not to resent the past; it may have been a great teacher. Just move forward to release and forgive the past. Become the navigator of your ship and lead yourself somewhere you haven't been for a while, like that cove of peace. Let go of your anger and guilt, and heavy emotions that keep you from experiencing inner peace. Say out loud to yourself, "I forgive myself for _____ and for anything else I've blamed myself for." Ask for celestial help by saying, "Please help me release all anger and guilt from my mind, body, and emotions." Then feel the anger and guilt and let them go. In doing this, your future will be enlarged.

One more thing about anger: When others lash out at you with words or actions, they are fighting a battle with and about themselves. The Dalai Lama said, "Anger is the most debilitating emotion. Not only does it affect the person who is angry, but also everyone around them. When anger dominates someone's mind, we should feel only compassion for them. That way we will spare ourselves the trouble of reacting with aggression ourselves." Others' anger can affect us, but don't take ownership of their issue and their anger.

As I mentioned, some hurts take a while to heal or heal in waves over time. Once a wave is truly forgiven, do not keep revisiting it as this only pulls you back into its muck and mire. That initial forgiveness may be all that is needed, but if not, another wave will catch you out of the blue and ask you once again to go through to a deeper layer. Sometimes, there is no way of understanding the healing process.

Our future is not dependent on what we may have lived through or what we know, but on how well we can apply what we *know now*. With our knowingness, we can exhale "bitterness" and inhale "betterness." We release that *bitterness* into *betterness*, just by changing the vowel, just by changing the reaction. If we eventually forgive and let go, we change the *bitter* into the *better*. The past is the past and can no longer dictate who you are.

You can have your campfire of anger, but we need to extinguish it before we walk away or it could burn down the whole forest. One day, you will be free from the fire within, and past hurts and shortcomings of self and others will dissolve into the heart of God.

"Death is an illusion."
—Renee Salvatori

Death and Reincarnation

Like many of you, I have witnessed the deaths of close family members and friends, but no matter how many deaths I witnessed, I was still unsettled in my thoughts of death. I finally decided to make peace with death after two of my own near-death experiences. Those two profound incidences made me analyze life in a whole different light.

The first time I almost died, I was so feeble and sick I didn't know what was going on with my body. The antibiotic I was on for an infection was counteracting to the dental material that was being used in some extensive dental work. It was such an odd circumstance that neither physician nor dentist put the reaction of the two together. I was losing muscle coordination, couldn't eat, and could barely stand on my own two feet without support. I would go in every two days for IV therapy and to see the doctor. After three weeks, I finally collapsed. I was taken to the hospital and they finally figured it out. I stayed almost a week in the hospital on high doses of allergy medication, cortisone, and vitamin C until I was clear of all immediate danger; I lived on those high doses of vitamin C and allergy medication for another month after that. To say that those few weeks of struggling were scary is an understatement. I resolved to my physicality ending. Even though I had four small children and felt pained at the thought of leaving them, I couldn't imagine continuing to exist physically. Then my health began to improve over the next few months, and with each improvement came the resolve to keep finding more health.

I had no time to analyze my second near-death experience until I'd survived it. I had an anaphylactic reaction and awoke in the trauma unit extremely glad to be alive, and I only had thoughts of going home to be with my family. In that situation, I felt like Wilbur the pig in the cartoon movie, *Charlotte's Web* when he cried, "I don't want to die. I don't want to die."

From my two experiences, I've learned that if one has the luxury of contemplating living and dying, one may realize feelings toward both will change from day to day. At this point in my life, without any physical or mental pain and without a tired soul, I want to stay here and exist physically longer. However, having gone through my life changing episodes of being ready and not being ready to die, I am no longer afraid of death. My heart may never want to leave loved ones, but fear of doing so no longer overwhelms me.

I looked into death from religious and personal beliefs. I wanted to merge the two into my own complete understanding. This was a slow process, and I felt safe by considering it first from the religious aspect. I looked into the Bible. The ancient teaching of "I have a body, but I am not my body" was where I started to analyze. This proved a distinct separation to me. The body has more to its skin-deep analogy. There was much significance given to the soul in the scriptures as an individual energy. The body has many deaths, but the soul never experiences an ending like a death. The body can be buried, but the soul continues on. The soul has many different journeys. So if the body and the soul experience differences, what does this mean in terms of life and death? I likened it to a book. The book is a physical thing. You can hold it, see it, and smell it. It holds a great story. After you read it, the book may be closed and returned to the library, but you remember the story in a place the hands, eyes, and nose do not need to experience to understand or remember it. The book is out of sight, but the story is not out of mind. Our bodies are like that too in the physical death; stripped of pages, words, and binding, we are still the story that goes on and never ends. Our soul continues. We are that proverbial song "that never ends; it just goes on and on, my friends." Our body may no longer exist, but our soul/story always will, like a sweet lingering memory or that great story never to be forgotten.

In the Bible book of Psalms, death is not an end. The Jews, Hindus, Buddhists, and many others believe in a "beyond." There is so much proof to see and read if you need it, whether from the Bible or from stories today.

There are many people who have had near death experiences and come back to tell about them. Even little four-year-old children can tell you what they saw and felt in the beyond. Although science has proven these descriptions are not just dream state excursions, many people still feel descriptions of the beyond or an afterlife are mental delusions. To this I say, proof is only accepted by those that need it, but cannot be given to those that do not want it.

Once, I was trying to understand why there were so many differing reports of the beyond by those who tried to explain what they saw, felt, or heard. Why did some see streets of gold, some hear choirs of angels, and some immediately see loved ones who had passed away? Just like during our earthly days, we each are living our own lives in the most interesting and fulfilling ways we can. We are not all the same, and so we will experience differently not only our earthly life, but also our heavenly life. We do not become cookie-cutter beings once we have passed. We all choose our earthly moments and we will choose our heavenly moments as our own creations. Perhaps if family was very important to you, you may see them first. If you are comforted by angels, you may be welcomed by their choir. We don't stop creating once we pass into the heavenly realm.

A fact of living is that everything living will die or shed its earthly body. That may be hard to swallow, especially when we are feeling, like Wilbur the pig in *Charlotte's Web*, that death is imminent and against our wills, or we are feeling heavy with grief and not wanting to leave. No one gets off earth with their physical body, not Jesus, Gandhi, Mother Teresa, or you. We will all experience a passing, or shedding, of our physical coat of flesh and bones. That is the only death one truly experiences. The soul never dies but merely passes to the next performance or journey with a different costume and renewed excitement. My daughter once said earth felt like a vacation and heaven felt like home. She was only four when she analyzed this. Somehow and for some unknown reasons, we tend to forget this true scenario of earthly living. We forget why we truly came here for a visit, so to speak. Perhaps we become forgetful while forming so many attachments here.

Death can be like the family member or best friend who moves away to another state or another country. The one who is left behind usually mourns the most for the missing love and friendship. The one who moved is usually experiencing many new and exciting sensations, sights, sounds, and textures, and often she does not have the agony of loss the one who stayed experiences. The five senses of physical love are *seeing, smelling, hearing, tasting* and *touching* the loved one, and it is these five physical senses we miss. You will adjust to this gap of senses with time, tears, and memories filling the void. The heart of the matter is, separation hurts, and it can hurt beyond any physical pain you have ever felt. Death is saying good-bye to loved ones' physical book, but not to their stories. Not being able to hold that bound book, even if only for a little while, can feel like forever. That forever, called mourning or adjustment, is the sadness we will have.

Have you ever known someone who committed suicide? We can hold judgment and analyze profoundly until it makes us crazy, but the truth is that person chose to exit stage left when they had had enough of the theatre. Suicide is a shortened physical ending, but that is all. We deem their short exit as inappropriate because there was a killing, yet we are all killing our very own bodies slowly each and every day without judging ourselves harshly. We consume food and drinks we know are not healthy for our bodies; we take in drugs, polluted air, and negative thoughts. Killing ourselves slowly may not be as humane as a quick suicide. Slowly living, while consuming all sorts of items that will eventually kill the physical body, is death just the same. I am not condemning or recommending either direction; each is an individual choice, chosen by an individual soul. We have no way of knowing what anyone's prior choices were, just as others do not know our prior choices.

Just because we begin to understand death does not mean we should be stoic about it. We only need to make peace with death, ours or someone else's. Yes, we will cry for the unlived lives of the young, and we will cry for the lived lives of the old. We are humans with great emotions; we feel with every ounce of our beings. That is what our earthly experience is all about. That is why we choose to come and experience life in its totality. We may not fully understand or remember until we get to that other side, when the whole picture of our lifetimes is laid out and can again be viewed. Although we mourn a person's transition, we celebrate his or her life here on earth, knowing they are but temporarily missed.

Death and life are of equal but contrasting importance. If the temperature on the thermometer reads 52 degrees, it is 52 degrees. If you are just coming out of the hot days of summer, 52 degrees will feel cold, and you may bundle up. If you are just coming out of the cold days of winter, you may feel 52 degrees is very warm and enjoyable. Your reaction will depend on how your skin and body adjusts to the temperature, and your opinion about 52 degrees will be influenced by the season you are leaving. Death is like this, too. Death is death. If you are going to death from earthly living, you may view it as scary. If, however, you are looking back at death after crossing over, you may view it as refreshing. We all need to find the peace we need…with 52 degrees or with death.

Now, what are your thoughts about reincarnation? I find comfort in that word, like my kids found comfort in the idea of a "do-over" when a basketball shot didn't go as expected and they would take the shot again. I like the thought of getting to come back, not because I didn't get it right the first time, but because I get the freedom of choice and creativity once more. Who among us do not like the ability to create to her heart's content?

Living and dying are choices we often forget we have consciously made. Life on earth, with all its wonderful physical attributes, is an awesome experience that we personally have chosen to come and experience, and we can choose over and over again to experience many different things here. "All the world's a stage," Shakespeare said, and we get to choose which play we want to see and which acts we wish to take part in. We also get to choose when we wish to exit stage left or right. Just knowing you can experience life over and over again can take some of the intensity, or seriousness, out of life and death. If, however, you are afraid of hell from a religious belief, or your personal beliefs lead you to feel your life has not been a good one, you will naturally be afraid of death. If you don't believe in hell and purgatory, then you won't see your passing as a scary event. Some even believe that the body and soul are buried until a specific time, called the Resurrection, when Jesus returns and calls for all good people to awake. Your thoughts and perceptions of death and/or reincarnation may bring you comfort or discomfort. It is important to make peace with death, no matter what religion or upbringing you had.

If you feel your soul journeys throughout multiple lifetimes to experience many aspects of living, you may understand death not as an end but as a continuation. Death is the circle that seems to end but really has no beginning or end. Each earthly life you experience makes little stops or markings in the circle, but you and your lives are one continual loop. We only need remember death will always be a part of our circle. If you've seen *The Lion King*, you can get a visual when the new lion cub is held up and "The Circle of Life" is played. Life is ebb and flow, or a constant coming and going. Whatever our personal beliefs may be, we need to stop judging our own eventual death or the death of others as bad. Trust that everyone on a deep soul level knows their purpose and where they are in this circle.

In ancient times, priests and other religious leaders didn't want to encourage the idea of reincarnation. The very thought of a do-over left them feeling vulnerable in their attempts to manipulate and control the masses. They also feared a slacking society of sinners who would just wait to try harder in the next lifetime. Religious leaders pushed the one lifetime deal and the sin-punishment penalty hard. This all had to come from a very high source, like God, to be believed. Thus was invented the very human doctrine of hell, purgatory, permanent death, and confession for everything imaginable. Hell was for people who couldn't pay their way out of badness, and purgatory was for those whose families could pay churches money to say prayers or masses to shorten their loved ones' time sentenced there. Heaven was a one-time fulfillment to be earned in one *perfectly* lived life. Those who believed in an earthly resurrection had to wait in that permanent sleep-like death to see if their name was on the wake up or call-back list. You have to agree, these are some very inventive ways for yet more control. These doctrines were supposedly given to high-priests directly from God and were considered just as good as God's own word. Like those political campaigns today that say, "This is ____ and I approved this message," God may never have approved some of the messages posted by priests or scribes, but they spread like wildfire, and they are still being used today. Now, if in your earthly experience, you wish to have your life fulfilled by those belief patterns, God always allows our free-willed choices. Remember, your earthly and heavenly creations are respected by God, so you can have the fulfillment you need in your creating self. If, on the other hand, you wish to understand God's ease, you can lightly listen with your heart and not with the heavy hand of religion.

The soul itself has and may continue to wish for many growth experiences throughout eons of time. The purpose of each new life is to evolve further and move on to another level. The soul forever retains its higher growth patterns within and renews and updates them at new points in time. This brings the soul more enhanced aspects of *all* the patterns you have ever been or lived.

Sometimes we just cannot remember these many lives we have lived. I used to get exasperated because I couldn't remember mine, until one day I realized I couldn't even remember what I ate for breakfast nine hours earlier! While you might be interested to know what happened in your past lives, some of what happened just doesn't need to be remembered in your current life. The details may be unimportant, or they may be too depressing or too ego boosting. If continually think about our pasts, it may also keep us from enjoying this single life experience we are currently striving to enjoy. If remembering the past can somehow help you understand or enhance your now experience, then proceed slowly and enjoy, but be quick to stop if remembering makes you feel too vulnerable. Some can remember their pasts or have others help them in remembering. Just don't become too anchored in the past, which can keep you from moving freely in today. We only need to remember that our goal in this lifetime is to create love and help all mankind, no matter what our sordid pasts may be.

Reincarnation offers us wonderful spaces in time to rest or grow. You will await a perfect heavenly configuration that will once again offer you a perfect energy package to assist you in your continual forward evolution. Then, you can encounter new experiences that will again be exhilarating.

Find comfort and healing with death in your religious or spiritual faith. Until you can hold your loved ones again, hold them in your heart and memory. Even though you are not physically holding them anymore, your hold can be just as strong. Some people even bridge the astral world to the earthly world and communicate in a higher vibration. You may even begin to do this yourself out of a deep longing to communicate once again. I have heard of people who never thought this kind of communication was possible until their desire to find a new communication technique became very strong. You may personally have that gift or you may enlist the help of another to share his gift with you. This can be an awesome healing moment only if the healer who is conveying the conversation is doing so in pure love and genuineness. Be aware of charlatans who offer to communicate to others for you; not everyone's motives are pure.

At the end of your physical life, it is not a letting of life but simply the enjoyment of everything from the deepest level of all your lives ever lived.

Open Your Heart to the True You

Life and death are both part of the same unending experience. We are all that is, all that ever was, and all that ever will be. It is the world without end. God always says, "Welcome home," whether it is in a physical state or heavenly state.

*"Men honor what lies within the
sphere of their knowledge,
but do not realize how dependent
they are on what lies beyond it."*
—Chuang Tzu

Soul and Spirit

Many, me included, have interchanged the words soul and spirit. It is very easy to do. Throughout history, from culture to culture, and from differing religions, there are different shades of meaning in each of their definitions. Though there seems to be a division between them in our culture, there is much commonality. Both are unseen. We all know we have one even if it cannot be dissected or identified in a laboratory. Each has references to life and the invisible internal force that makes us human. We all agree that an inner consciousness inhabits each of us. Cultures call this internal force or consciousness by many names, but it is still the essence that identifies us and makes us who we are.

Terminology can be so fixed that it can block us because we get caught up in it. If you cannot get past a word, pick at least five other words that say the same thing for you. Find the word that most resonates and helps you understand the concept you are describing. If *soul* and *spirit* mean the same thing to you, use them as one and the same. You only need to feel the essence of the concept; you shouldn't let the terminology hang you up.

If you choose to read further, I will try to explain, with my limited knowledge as best I can, how some people distinguish the words one from another. Please understand this may also be my misinterpreted truths. So if my explanation leaves you confused, please keep searching for definitions that work easily for you. *Soul* refers to the whole person, life, and very essence or quality of you that identifies you as you. You are identified as a human soul, while your pet dog is identified as an animal soul. The soul refers to a human, all that is inside and that which provides a moral compass. Man is not a spirit but a soul who has a spirit. The soul is what gives your physical body its puppet strings or actions, so to speak. *Spirit* represents your disposition or personality, free-will, emotions, and your true evolved self. Part of God's spirit or spark is alive and in each and every one of our souls, no matter whom you are. God's spirit and your spirit are one. Think of the salutation "Namaste." It means, "The God (Spirit) in me recognizes and honors the God (Spirit) in you." Your soul or spirit represents your higher self and can travel astral planes. The physical body is earthbound and will die, while your spirit/soul lives forever.

Here is an example. You may be standing in a garden looking at many different flowers. To your right are roses and to your left are honeysuckles. They are both flowers, or flower souls. The scent of each group of flowers represents the spirit. The spirit of each flower is what makes one smell like a honeysuckle and the other, a rose. Our spirit is our flower scent, so to speak, our personality, our drive, and our resolve. Our souls can house a spirit of quiet, loud, quick, or demure characteristics, to name but a few possibilities.

Have you ever watched the animated movie *Spirit*? It is about the U.S. government's capture and training of horses to use building railroads. One horse in the group had a very feisty spirit and refused to be saddled and caged. The whole herd is a "group of horse souls," but each horse within that group had its own type of spirit. That certain horse was full of spirit while others might say the feisty horse was full of *soul*, just as if you were listening to a B.B King or Tina Turner song. Can you see how the words have been interchanged to the point many wonder if soul and spirit truly are interchangeable? Again, I say go with what the words' essences hold for you.

Some envision the soul as contained inside the body, although many now understand it is the other way around, and the body is inside the soul. Both soul and spirit extend beyond the physical form of the being. The soul cannot be contained or neatly packaged inside the body. It is much too big and expansive. I once read an analogy describing the soul as being like the air we breathe. The air not only surrounds us, but also is in us. Think of the air within a house; we may feel that each room's air is different. One room may feel stuffy, one room may be cool and airy, and one room may be aromatic with food smells. The air in each room feels different, yet it is all the same air circulating in the house. The air carries different properties, but it all merges and mingles effortlessly as one. Our uncontained souls are like that, too.

You can also look at soul like a mold, a candy mold, or a car engine mold. Our body is the poured substance, but our soul is the mold and its contents. Think of how many people can touch another with a smile or a look in their eyes. You can reach out and touch someone without physically touching someone. These are soulful touches that don't need to be experienced with physical hands. Your soul is beyond you. That's why touch and conversation are not the only ways to communicate. Our souls are free-floating, mingling effortlessly. When you sleep, the soul has the ability to remove itself from the density of the physical body and refresh itself, even though you may not have any memory of it in the morning.

If you've ever experienced an emotional heart matter like love, you know the feeling comes from the heart, yet you also feel it in other places throughout the body. You may feel it in the pit of your stomach, in your lungs through your breathing, or in a tingling sensation throughout your body. To label the feeling as only coming from the heart would have you running to doctors for examinations to explain your stomach and breathing issues and the weird sensations in your extremities. How could the heart pose all kinds of other body part awakenings? The soul and spirit are like a heart. Who knows where one will truly experience the meaning of them? Soul and spirit cannot be contained just as love cannot be contained to only the heart region.

The website www.differencebetween.net briefly compares the words soul and spirit by religion and by culture and breaks it down into easy references. Both words express an invisible force we carry with us daily, and remember, merging those shades of grey to experience and understand soul and spirit can be helpful. In fact, you don't even need to distinguish between them. Just feel their essence and enjoy them.

*"Like gravity, karma is so basic we
often don't even notice it."*
—Sakyong Miphan

Karma

Nowadays, karma seems to hold a lot of negative undertones. The word has Hindu and Buddhist origins and is defined as a person's actions having ethical consequences in determining their destiny in their next existence. Most western beliefs hold that karma is experienced immediately; that going to heaven or hell right after death is a consequence of their good or bad actions on Earth. Either way, karma is understood as your own goodness or badness that comes back to you. But why has the word *karma* become so negative rather than encouraging?

Humans cast judgment and punish in an attempt to hold ourselves and others accountable for our actions. Briefly think of how we do this with others. Maybe you have used the phrase, "Can't wait till her karma comes." "God will handle that and make them see." "What comes around goes around." How about "An eye for an eye," from the Bible? Many times I have uttered one or more of those statements to ease the pain I have felt in being wounded. Our pure spirits, which are always light, know we should love others even when we have been wronged, yet our egos just won't let us agree. Thus, we are thrown into conflict because those karmic statements feel so good and appear to heal our wounds and soothe our egos, yet we know we shouldn't judge. When we retaliate with karmic statements, our words have major undertones of both judgment and punishment, but karma is neither of these, and more importantly, these emotions are not from God.

We know God never holds a grudge, only humans do. We know God never wishes evil upon others, only our own hurts and angers do. If God knows the number of hairs on our heads or that a little sparrow has fallen, do you really think God wants to see another human fall on his face or experience retribution at the hands of his brother? We sometimes forget, but God is a God full of grace and mercy. God is the most forgiving light in the world and allows us to come in with a clean slate if we desire to. We may choose a better understanding of a situation from the life we are living or a life we have lived, but God never punishes to convince or correct past wrongs. Nor is our wanting a deeper understanding of something a debt that needs to be paid.

One more thing on judgment; "Judge not, lest ye be judged." When we judge another, our very judgment creates more karma. Judging will come back in the degree and intensity it was given out. Also, it is not wise to attach ourselves to another's learning patterns. I believe that is what was referenced to in the scripture of "an eye for an eye." We may never understand what is going on in another's mind because we are all on different levels of understanding and can never know what wisdoms another has gained. Pay attention to what you are trying to evolve into without attachment to others karma or realizations. Bless, bless, bless them, and keep moving on.

There is also the law of "cause and effect" that affects everything in creation. It is the "responsibility principle" that every action causes a reaction. It is "creations polarity". If you punch someone, he may punch you back or you may have to pay for dental work so the other person can get broken teeth fixed. If you speed, you may crash or get a ticket. If you litter, you may get fined. If you eat junk food, you will be unhealthy. If you drink excessive alcohol, you will become an alcoholic. When you smile at a person, you trigger niceness, and in return, he smiles back. If you hold open a door for a person, that person often holds the next set of doors open for you. If you scowl at someone, you can bet the other person will not offer a smile in return. The causes you create will affect others and yourself. In its simplest form, this is the "law of attraction," "cause and effect," and what some refer to as "karma."

Most of these "you get what you give out" statements are usually experienced in an *unconscious*, mindless, everyday living, on autopilot state. Karma on a truly conscious level is going through life *consciously* making many efforts to understand, to be love to all living things, and to evolve into your highest potential. Every moment of your life, you are creating karma, a day to day and lifetime to lifetime accomplishment. Today, you bombed as a parent, felt too negatively, or ate badly. Tomorrow, you are aware of issues and strive to yell less at your family, eat less junk food, or attain a higher ideal from yesterday. Sometimes, that tomorrow ends up being postponed until another time.

Karma is neither forceful nor thrown on us by others, including God. It is a loving, positive, and useful nudge in an area you personally wish to understand, but that is all. Karma changes a specific energy into a positive experience to match your pure soul. We are all good, even if that goodness is hard to locate at times. Our compass is always pointed due north, and even when we gravitate to other points of interests and desires that may not be beneficial to ourselves or others, eventually we all can be pointed back on course. That is karma, a striving to advance into a higher state of understanding, getting back on track by using our internal compass to reach our own North Star. Some may postpone their understanding until another lifetime, while some need several lifetimes to get redirected. Some may hesitate for different reasons: not wishing to understand now, no longer needing to understand, or because of one's inability to understand just yet. Your soul will always serve you well and stand ready to help you find your North Star when you are ready. It is every soul's longing. The soul is like the little old two-inch toys from Playskool called Weebles. You might remember the advertising slogan, "Weebles wobble but they don't fall down." No matter how many times you tried to knock them over or hold them down, they would always pop back up without fail. You just couldn't hold a Weeble down. Our soul is like the Weeble. It will always strive to right itself no matter how many times your physical body tries to hold it down.

Our karma or understanding can be gentle or as powerful and drawn-out as we wish. Some people have a hard time forgiving themselves and so choose to punish themselves and others in ways they personally deem fit. Remember, karma is never punishment but only an understanding. Think of how two exercise coaches can believe in two different exercise techniques. One will say, "No pain, no gain," while the other says, "Take it nice and slow and do not strain." Just as you choose your exercise coach, you choose your understanding styles. Pain and punishment deemed necessary are one's own personal creations. You choose to learn in gentleness or harshness, and you choose to grasp your karma immediately or carry it into other lifetimes until you decide you no longer need to punish yourself.

Years ago, my son was upset over purchasing a toy and had buyer's remorse. I explained that perhaps next time he could think about a purchase for a few days before rushing to buy it. Later, we went for ice cream, but he didn't want to go. He said he didn't deserve ice cream because he'd spent money on a stupid toy. For me, this really drove home the fact that people needlessly punish themselves. I wasn't angry with him and had only offered some insight to future purchases knowing how he was feeling. He, on the other hand, felt the need to punish himself. He quickly worked his punishment out when I mentioned he could get sprinkles, but others may not be as easily convinced! Having insight on a matter is usually the only "karmic light" needed to resolve a problem. Like shining a flash light under a bed to find the dropped jewelry that bounced there, sometimes we drop our common sense and lose our way, and we merely have to shine a light to find it again. Some don't see that "easy" solution as enough, though, so their minds will trick them and make them pay endlessly for having had the problem. Pain and punishment are our own creations, just as understanding is allowed through us. You choose what you need.

Sometimes the only thing needed to enable a longing for improvement is to forgive oneself and others. That may be the only karmic lesson or stepping stone needed for higher growth. Think of a parent who yells at her child, only to later hug the child and apologize. How about the person who earlier cut you off in traffic, but later regrets his action? How about that person who stole but later returned the item? My brother was misdiagnosed from an x-ray which perhaps resulted in his early death. My parents sat across from the physician as he apologized and acknowledged he had learned from this oversight and would use this new knowledge in treating other children. My parents were completely crushed to have lost a son, but they also chose to forgive the physician. I hope that physician has also been able to forgive himself for his mistake. In realization and forgiveness, karma can be released. Once you realize you no longer want or need a learning experience, at any moment, you can erase the karmic pattern of it. I've heard it said there is nothing wrong with making a mistake; only ignoring the mistake is a mistake. If we ignore and cannot eventually forgive ourselves or others, we are not necessarily de-evolving, but we are not evolving either. We are flat-lining. Truly forgiving requires karmic resolve to recall those who hurt you and feel the power to wish them well. Our current goal is to keep moving forward and to learn from the peaks and valleys on our humanness monitor.

Again, when we are eager to understand something, it always changes the energy involved into a positive force. Think of it this way. Say in a past life I did not have self-esteem, and so I determined in my next life I wanted to work further on self-esteem. This karma or low self-esteem issue would only be stretching me to enhance myself into a healthier expression of who I am. Another example is if I felt I let someone down in a past expression of myself, and I wanted to come back and further express myself into a better feeling.

When we come to earth, we become full of emotion and many dense bodily functions. An emotion felt in its totality or denseness may be longed for once again in an earthly experience, so we can completely express ourselves. Again, it is our choosing and no one else's, just as we choose our own learning styles. A drug pusher who may have ruined many lives financially or physically may decide to come back in his next life to work with addicted bodies or to experience financial hardship himself. He may already be highly aware and remorseful over how his actions affected others and may not need to experience anything else regarding this, unless he wishes to experience it.

Karma is like laundry sitting by the washing machine. Without attention, the laundry will continue to pile up until we realize we need clean underwear and jeans. Even then, we may ignore the laundry and purchase new clothes. Sometime in another life, you may decide to take the laundry bull by the horns and learn how to do it.

Karma and cellular memories are two different things. We experience this life as a singular experience, even though we carry all aspects of the many other lives we've lived in our conscious and unconscious memories and cells. Cellular memories may come with much intensity or without even the slightest recognition, as if a speck of dust had landed on your hair. Hopefully, these memories will not come to you as guilt, but as a remembrance of what was. Like those paper certificates that hang on your wall confirming your completion of a class, memories may serve as earthly reminders of a life once completed.

Memories are like looking at a photograph today and remembering the period of time surrounding that moment. The photograph may bring happiness or sadness. With a cellular memory from another lifetime, we can experience joy, sweetness, fear, anger, or sadness. The negative feelings usually get our attention because when you are feeling good, and then a second later that happy feeling ends with a different memory, and you are brought to your knees, you definitely pay attention. Just as with a photograph, we may not need to do anything but look at the snapshot. Cell memories can be tricky to navigate since they can feel like not just a snapshot, but like an overwhelming, full-color, flashing billboard sign.

An example of this for me was with an acupuncture session. One day I panicked halfway through the session and was mentally planning my escape. I tried to remember how many needles the acupuncturist had placed and where they all were, so I could take them out and sneak down the back stairs. I was overcome with such fear and dread that beads of sweat were pouring out of me. I did not make my escape, though, and after the therapist took the needles out, I was on my way. I got to the car and sobbed. I truly didn't understand what had happened because, during many years of treatment, I had always felt so relaxed during sessions, and I completely trusted this person. Later, I spoke with an energy healer who helped me understand what had happened. This healer explained a cell memory had been triggered. Up until that day, I was unaware of such things as cellular memory. My cells were having a flash back, or seeing a snapshot, so to speak, of a past life where I was experimented upon. Even though I had no visuals of it in my mind, my cells held the memory and had decided to share it with me at that moment. Cell memories do not necessarily mean karma, but I needed to understand what had happened, so I enlisted the help of someone who explained that odd moment of out-of-proportion fear. I was now able to understand the complexity of cell memories. I initially had an emotion over that snapshot, but I burned it later, like an old lover's photograph.

Cell memories can be positive, too. I love certain smells of flowers and feel like I melt into a different world when I smell them. In a later energy class, I found out that, in one of my lifetimes, I'd worked with flowers. It was fine for me not to understand why I enjoyed flowers, and I never searched out the reason for enjoying those particular smells. That casual revelation only provoked a little "ah" moment.

If memories remembered, on your own or with the help of another, help you understand something or help you move forward—always forward—then they are beneficial. If they pull you down, and make you feel sad or guilt-laden, ask them to leave. Tell them they may have served you well in another lifetime, but they are no longer needed. Bless them and continue enjoying your new life. At the acupuncture session, I could have asked that memory to leave, but I truly didn't understand what cell memory was then. I only knew I'd hit panic mode, and I had no understanding why. Now that you understand what cell memory is, maybe you will not be blindsided as I was.

Once we get back to the other side or heaven, we can look at all our lives' journeys and decide if there is anything we wish to experience for understanding and clarity or if we wish to experience life anew. Remember, we are creators of our lives' experiences. We may find that hard to comprehend and feel we are merely innocent bystanders, but it is this unconsciousness that makes us complacent in life, and leads us to forget to create and keep evolving forward.

We sit looking at the white canvas on the easel and forget what we may dream of being, creating, or forgiving. We are here to create wonderful things in great love. I did not say big things. We cannot all be Wilbur and Orville Wright or a Ben Franklin. Whether you are tying your child's shoelaces, cooking dinner, or holding a friend's hand, you are doing small things with great love. A nuclear physicist could have a great and high ranking job and hold a grand fancy title, but if he does not follow through with love, he may create a bomb big enough to annihilate us all. Greatness is not as important as love.

God is a God of love and joy, not regrets or burdens for us to see the error of our ways. Karma is not a replaying of what was, and it should not be a falling back to an experience, especially one you may wish to forget. We are all evolving, and if we are pulled back continually, we will not be moving ahead. We will be de-evolving, or becoming less than we have attained. Our life's purpose is to evolve to a higher level of love and understanding. Also, if we come into our new body in a new lifetime with love as our highest intention, we won't need to make anything right from past lives. Our awareness of love and goodness projected to all trumps past karma. When I say to come in with a deep love for others, I do not mean dreamily catching butterflies in a meadow or throwing coins into every corner tin can, but having a deep love for self, for others, and for animals and plants. It can also mean extending a form of tough love to family or friends when needed, and it could also mean allowing others to love you in return. All love is a giving and a taking.

As we evolve, we are trying to create a space of love for ourselves and everyone else. So the karmic push is always to create in love and be love. The Hindu scriptures say, "As the blazing fire reduces wood to ashes, similarly, the fire of self-knowledge reduces all karma to ashes." Life truly can resolve itself in the process of life. The theologian James Freeman Clarke said, "Seek to do good, and you will find that happiness will run after you." You can't steer yourself wrong if you travel in love and goodness through the lifetime you are experiencing.

Think of all those wonderful little souls born so pure and eagerly waiting to start life with gusto. If these little babies knew they were coming to pay off many debts, do you think they would come in so ready to experience the world and the harsh reality of what they created in another lifetime? They are only eager to experience a clean slate and a wonderful opportunity for love and creativity.

God is a God of joy, not regrets, burdens, or karmic pay-offs. The word *karma* has come to have a scary connotation when it is merely a learning tool for evolving in this lifetime or any other. Karma should only be associated with thoughts of higher understanding, serving as a stepping stone. Again, your soul may only need understanding, love, or a forgiving release to change your energy. That is the basis of karma and is so very basic to understanding.

"Out of the ashes rises the phoenix."
—Unknown

Negatives into Joy

Joy cannot be faked. It is hard to act joyful when you aren't because it makes you feel divided inside. Oh, the outer smile can be faked, but not the true "feel it in your soul" joy. You can smile at yourself and others and give yourself great affirmations with joyful words, but that is only the outward appearance of joy. There is more to feeling it in your soul than lip service. We can keep faking it until we can make it, but we all want to get past the pretend stage.

It is easy to be positive and happy when things go well. The bills don't exceed the bank account; there is no physical pain and illness; there are no big conflicts in life. At other times, though, it is extremely challenging to find joy, especially when you are in discomfort because discomfort pulls your attention to the lack of positive feelings. If that isn't enough, you still need to deal with other people who have their own issues, which can prove to be extremely difficult.

We grow tired, weary, and beaten down with everyday living. The world bombards us with more negatives than positives, so we have to work harder at maintaining good feelings. I heard a wonderful statement once that gave me hope. "The world is the worst it has ever been, but it is also the best it has ever been." Even when I am upset over an incident, I try to see something else that encourages me and confirms the world is indeed a good place. We decide where to rest our attention. Which playground of thought would you rather have? When I look at the world through what is considered rose-colored glasses, I feel more hopeful and positive.

A good deal of help can be given by self-talk, affirmations, and placing oneself in and around people who look at the glass as half-full. There may be times when you are feeling blue or are in a very rough spot. Those are the times to keep the self-help going and hang around things, places, or people who encourage you.

A man was experiencing a serious health issue with cancer. He decided to eliminate as many negatives as he could and surround himself with positives. He wasn't able to dump the cancer or the mounting bills, but he was able to change what he surrounded himself with. He turned off the negative news and television shows, talked to himself in positive ways, hung around positive people, and watched funny sitcoms like Abbott and Costello. This was all to his advantage because he was able to navigate his illness into recovery. This navigating was so successful he continued it even after the cancer was in remission.

Like that man who navigated his illness and finances, we too can reach for better and brighter things. He was sick and in pain physically but felt *hopeful* mentally. The difference between *pain* and *hopeful* is the recovery of the mind and body. Think how you want to feel, and perhaps you will feel how you think. Your attention to positives can get energy flowing. Work at feeling good mentally even while feeling bad physically. And the same can be reversed and said to work at feeling good physically while feeling bad mentally. I say "work" because it is work. You must pay constant attention to how you wish to manage your dilemma.

That man in our story worked at not living in the dilemma of his illness and began living in its resolution by placing himself into positive venues. When we have dilemmas, problems, or questions, eventually we need to move out of that stage and into the next phase of resolution and answer. Staying in the problem constantly is not advancing in any direction and leaves one bitterly stuck in the worst of places.

Here are a few examples. Dilemma: "I am so tired; I am always so tired." Resolution: "I am very tired, so I will rest more and not do too many extra things. Maybe I need to get to bed earlier." Can you see the differing approaches? One keeps you where you currently are, while the other puts you into forward gear. Here's another one. Dilemma: "I am always tired. There must be something wrong." Resolution: "I am always tired. I may need to go see a doctor, eat healthier, get some exercise, or cut down on some stresses." The dilemma phase leaves you wondering around in your head aimlessly, whereas the resolution phase takes you into a proactive direction. The initial dilemma is telling you something good because the problem now has your attention. You can stay in the problem phase or take action and try to resolve it. What if the first resolution you come up with doesn't work? Keep going until you hit on one that will. Forward mental thinking makes all the difference.

To be successful, you have to really focus on moving forward. Have you ever watched a basketball game where the player starts out in one direction only to suddenly stop, pivot on his foot, and go in another direction? When heading into a not-so-good place, we can choose to pivot as many times needed to head into better thoughts. There are pockets in my life in which I really have to work hard at pivoting my thoughts over and over again. Some days, my friend, it is truly very hard. If you watch the players in a basketball game, you see them sweating and breathing heavily. In our basketball game of life, we may work very hard, too.

If pivoting doesn't help, try another approach. There are times I have to ask myself two questions: "What am I happy for?" and "If tomorrow doesn't come, how can my today be great?" Those two questions help me find joy in holding a hand longer, giving extra kisses to my family, apologizing for something, singing off-key, thanking someone, or giving a compliment just because. Sometimes, I still have to open all the blinds to see the sunshine while I continue to dig very deep to find one thing I am happy about. It may take a while, but once I harness one joy, it's as if a magnet has been attached to it, and more joys get pulled in.

Go slow and look for one small thing a day to be happy about. Most people can find joy on a week's vacation or a dinner night out, but can you find joy in otherwise simple, everyday things? Think of yourself on a treasure hunt of joy. What may be waiting to be added to your treasure chest? Great tasting coffee, a sunny day, a day off, a stirring book, an unfolding rose, a child's laughter, a good movie, or a bird's song? Once you get the joy search going, it builds momentum amazingly quickly, like the momentum that builds while going down a hill on a sled or giggling when tired as each little thing becomes funnier and funnier. How about your new love interest that grows stronger and stronger or that one bite of a potato chip that leads to more because you can't just stop at one?

Once momentum is going, there is an ease in moving forward. The words *moment* and *momentum* are very close in their Latin origin, which is interesting because how many of us can find momentum building in each moment to moment experience? Whether we are angry or joyful, momentum can build. When angry in the moment, it can lead to yet more anger. When joyful in the moment, it, too, can lead to more joy.

Joy may not be easy at times or even attainable some days, or at certain seasons of your life. However, if you can hit on one single joyful moment, you may encourage another joyful moment out of momentum and then another, and yet another. Maybe then the momentum to joy will have an ease to it. Try it! Be joyous over your bed and pillow. Be happy you have a warm shower to envelope you. The clothing you choose in the morning and your cereal preferences will be fun. Your pets antics will make you laugh instead of yell. The traffic will give you time to collect your thoughts. The rude associate will make you happy you learned politeness. The burned dinner will become funny as you pour your second meal of the day from yet another box of cereal. Before you know it, you may have many moment to moment joys in the day, week, year, and even for longer periods of your life. From the shirttails of momentum, joy will feel like it is coming from the deepest parts of you.

Finding your positive momentum does not mean finding major over-the-top moments. That would be like going to Disney World when you really didn't feel like being happy and navigating a sea of smiling, enthusiastic people. Maybe a better choice would be to go to the local park where you can sit, be in the fresh air, and watch the goings-on. You are reaching out but in a more attainable way. Another positive option may be staying away from an overwhelming party and getting a funny, feel-good movie and watching it at home alone or with a friend. Momentum starts with small steps and does not overwhelm.

Stop watching scary and discouraging news, television series, or movies. If you enjoy music, be a wise D.J. and direct the mood. Trade the down and woeful tunes for upbeat ones. There are many funny sitcoms to be found on television; you can also purchase many of them by the season. Shows like *I Love Lucy, The Big Bang Theory, Abbott and Costello*, or any you find upliftingly therapeutic are good options. Get some feel good reads in the comic/humorous section at the library or the book store. There are great comic books and novels. Every time I reread *The Shepherd, the Angel, and Walter the Christmas Miracle Dog*, I laugh out loud. Laugh your way into a good mood. Clean up as much negative debris as you can.

When you think of what your heart and lung muscles do for you, maybe you can understand how the brain is also capable of cleaning up our thoughts. One half of your heart takes in blood that needs cleaned up, and it pumps this blood to the lungs. Fresh blood with lots of oxygen now comes back from the lungs and is sent through your body by the second half of your heart. Your life force is now renewed and clean. Your brain can perform a similar kind of clean up. You will have negative thoughts, but you can filter them out just as quickly as your heart and lung muscles filter out debris from your blood. There is nothing wrong in thinking negative thoughts or letting them float through our brain like a passing internal cloud. Holding onto those thoughts is another story. They can come in, but we should clean them up. The heart has yet another amazing ability; there are tiny doors, or valves, that close so blood does not flow the wrong way during this process of cleaning the blood. We may need to completely close our mental valves to stop some negative thoughts from even getting in. If they do happen to get in, open the door and let them out. Can't you just picture yourself literally closing a door to a thought that is not beneficial? When you feel the pulse in your wrist or the beat of your heart, think, pulse = positive. What cleanup work can you do?

Keep telling yourself you are okay and you are successfully finding ways to achieve your positives. You are more equipped today than yesterday to direct your life. We all grow smarter every day because we have learned new tools and strategies. Someone I know uses the "power-suggestion" strategy. He goes around saying he is "great" *all the time*. He has quite a few medical issues and genuine concerns. It is his way of getting into a positive flow, but his wife gets upset at times because she needs to know how he is doing. Sometimes when we start being positive, it is like riding a bicycle for the first time; we are not quite sure how to stay up (positive) without falling, so we tend to overcompensate a little. It is okay to announce you are tired because that is a true statement, but you can also add, "But I'll feel more awake in a little while." First, be honest if you need to express your feeling, and then envision positives, both verbally and mentally. This is like pre-paving work. You are preparing and pre-paving for the positives or better moments ahead.

Here are a few more forward-moving suggestions. Can you incorporate some activity or thought which brings you joy even once a week? Hang around positive people, and shield yourself as much as you can from the Debbie-Downers of the world. No longer submit yourself to situations that negatively influence your life, even if you get five minutes of fun from it, for the negative baggage can last longer. Rework the voice inside your head to speak positively to yourself and others. Try to outwit all the negative words, feelings, or thoughts toward yourself and others. Give a compliment just because. Pick something that gets your blood pumping in a good way which may inspire and bring out your best side. All these little things will enhance your healing and recovery.

There is evidence that when you are kind to others, happiness and joy have a way of seeping in. Little kindnesses cost nothing but pay big dividends. You can be polite on the telephone to a marketer or sales associate, smile at someone in the checkout line, hold open a door, say thank-you, say goodnight, say hello, clean up litter in your neighborhood, or send a get-well card. These are all the tiniest actions, but they are more meaningful to you and others than you may realize.

Pick a role model for inspiration. Once, when I was at a low point, my role model was St. Nicholas. Yes, you read that correctly. Santa, as we now call him, was a real person who was born in the part of Greece that is today known as Turkey. He didn't live in the North Pole, have flying reindeer or elves, or carry a magic sack, but he was a real person who gave in other ways. At the time, I still felt burned by religion, faith, and God, but I needed a joyful person I could emulate. He was a man who modeled a generous heart by dropping coins into the windows of needy families' homes and helping the sick and suffering when he could. I admired his actions. Through those years of reaching for my positives, I did as many little secret Santa gifting as I could as I attempted to steer away from my own negative thoughts and work into other positives. Each recovery and healing time is individual, so pick the Rx or healing program you need. You are your own physician here.

Sometimes even our best intentions aren't making the strides we envision. Don't judge yourself because then you will become more attached to the slowness of your progress, and guilt will make you feel worse. Try your best not to judge your thoughts and emotions. If you slam the judge's gavel down on yourself, your judgment holds you down instead of pushing you up. By all means, please allow yourself some feeling down times. We are entitled to these. There may be days where the clouds settle in low and stay for a while. Let them be your friend and ask what they are telling you. Are they telling you some redirection in your living style, relationships, health, job, or thoughts are needed? Are those clouds telling you joy cannot be obtained on your own? Maybe you need help navigating a difficult time or perhaps there is a chemical imbalance that needs assistance from a physician to be righted. Do not feel embarrassed or ashamed to enlist help! Helping hands extended when we are in need are wonderful. Be light on judgment and guilt when you seek help or when you spend time with your dark clouds so you can hear what they are telling you.

Don't expect people, money, or health to make you happy. You can be handed all the money in the world or all the health in the universe, but you cannot hang your happiness on these things; if you do, you will then find something else to be upset about, like your job, your partner, your kids, or the weather.

Plant your own happiness seed, water it, pull the weeds, nurture it, and enjoy your harvest. Then and only then, will happiness come from the inside out. You may not have a perfect life, but there are ways around this imperfection. A successful man is one who can lay a firm foundation with what life has thrown at him, or, in other words, only the choice to be happy causes happiness.

Remember the joke about Moses? He started out as a basket case, and God made something of him. Ask Divine Beings (God and Angels) for the highest and best outcome for the day ahead. Ask that only positive energy surround you. Be comforted that help is available to you. Think of a child tying her shoes. That child may try and try and try. She won't allow help because she wants to do it herself. Finally, after much effort, she asks for help. Your help is only the first step. Her allowing you to help is the next step. Picture that same child asking for help, but constantly pulling her feet away. She is asking but not really accepting. How many of us, like that child, ask for help yet do not allow it? None of us is ever beyond help of Celestial Heavens, friends, family, or doctors.

Many times we can find encouragement from unexpected places. My sister enjoys the song, "Put One Foot in Front of the Other" sung by Mickey Rooney and Keenan Wynn from the 1970's cartoon movie, *Santa Claus is*

Coming to Town. Maybe you can listen to or read the words sometime and feel their positive motivation.

There is an old Native American folk tale of a Cherokee grandfather teaching his grandson about life. "Inside each of us are two wolves that constantly fight. One of the wolves is positive and is filled with peace, calm, love, and kindness. The other wolf is negative and filled with fear, anxiety, self-pity, and self-doubt." The boy asked the grandfather, "If the wolves are always fighting, which one of them will win?" The grandfather replied, "The one that you feed the most." Feed the positive wolf in you. Eventually the negative one will wither away. This is also the same formula for our strengths and weaknesses. When we give attention to our weakness, we become weaker. When we give attention to our strengths, we become stronger. This is also true of how we see others. If we see them as weak, they will be weak. If we see them as strong, they will be strong. We continue on to wellness and joy when we proceed from wellness and joy.

When you feel good or start feeling good, it is wise not to feel guilty about it, especially if those around you are still feeling badly. We are allowed every single piece of happiness, even when say our friend is sick or our neighbor's house just burned down. Do you understand what I mean? You cannot get sick enough or negative enough to make others' sicknesses or negatives go away. You cannot get poor enough, financially or mentally, to make others rich. Enjoy what goodness you have. This is your life and happiness. Allow and enjoy both without guilt.

Happiness is not a destination a person reaches but simply a way of traveling. Let your mind and body relax into your travels. Happiness is not "out there somewhere;" it is attainable today. See you, your life, and your today as you want it. Redirect yourself into the positives and joy you desire. When people tell you to face your reality and be a realist, don't listen unless that is exactly how you wish it to be. Create your reality, no matter how silly it seems. There is no one set way to finding positives, and you will have to find what works for you. Once you do, many obstacles will fall away, and you will feel true joy and happiness in the very deepest part of very soul.

> *"Just because you're not sick doesn't mean you're healthy."*
> —Renee Salvatori

Energy Medicine

Energy medicine, which can stem from Eastern or Western tradition, is not a physical medicine you take from a bottle or package. Most energy medicines are modernized, but all of them stem from ancient practices of bringing health naturally to the body. Our ancient ancestors used these natural and instinctual techniques for healing themselves and others, and they thrived. These ways are the safest and most organic forms of healing. Many people are now stepping back into these harmonious ways.

Energy is a powerful force within and around us. Your body's energies are always working. When your energy is in harmony, you naturally feel better. When your energies are short-circuiting, your energies will not be in harmony, and physical and mental health will be hindered. Bear in mind, the energy medicines I speak of here can be used in conjunction with your medical practitioner. One does not need to replace the other.

You have heard people say thoughts are powerful, and this is true because thoughts are energy. Some understandable examples of thought energy are prayer and love/light thoughts. When you are holding or are given these energies, you naturally feel the benefits. There is no time in space, and space does not have geographical boundaries. You can send this energy on any day or at any time. Again, since thoughts are energy, it is important to keep thoughts of a positive nature toward ourselves or others. We never want to hold onto negative energy since there is no benefit to it.

Forms of energy movement you can learn include tai chi, Qi Gong, yoga, meditation, chakras, meridians and radiant circuits, massage, color therapy, crystal therapy, and reflexology (acupressure). As you begin to learn, you may need the help and guidance of a certified or experienced energy healer.

Reflexology is applying pressure to the feet, hands, or ears. The International Institute of Reflexology (www.reflexology-usa.net) offers further information, as well as lists of certified reflexologists. You can also find information at www.littleephihany.com, www.reflexologyscience.com, or www.how-to-do-reflexology.com. Charts show areas of the feet, hands, or ears and what body parts are affected when pressure is applied to those areas. The charts show where nerve endings are. I use a foot chart to help me locate where I should apply pressure. For example, if I have a sinus issue, I look at the chart to see where to apply pressure or where to rub my feet to bring relief to the sinus area. Although this self-practice is helpful, sometimes I schedule an appointment with a certified reflexologist to get a complete tune-up. Another great self-help is the Donna Eden methods, which teach you how to direct your own energy for healing and well-being. Donna Eden had tuberculosis as a child, multiple sclerosis as an adolescent, and a heart attack in her twenties. Because of her health issues, Eden pushed to find ways of healing herself, including searches of ancient healing methods. In her work, Eden shares many easy and "do-it-yourself" ways to health. Her pamphlet, "The Five Minute Daily Energy Routine," demonstrates exercises so easy I hesitate to call them exercises. You can do them anywhere while standing, sitting, or lying down. Eden developed her methods with ease as a primary component because she wants everyone to be able to experience health in the simplest and easiest fashion.

Eden feels that when you don't feel good in your body, you can't accomplish much. These easy techniques will begin to give you your health and stamina back; you can then make choices from the radiant health that is your birthright. Eden has made her techniques available in many ways: CDs, DVDs, YouTube.com presentations, her website, and books. Eden's books may appear big and overwhelming, but sections can be picked out and read as needed. If you still feel unsure, you can find certified healers on her website who will help you with the techniques.

Have you ever felt worse after exercise instead of energized? In Eden's DVD, *Introduction to Energy Medicine*, she explains why this can happen and she demonstrates how to reset your energy to move forward instead of backward. When you exercise, or even walk while your energy is moving backward, you will only feel worse. She teaches a one-minute technique to change that backward pattern, so instead of feeling zapped, you will feel energized while walking or exercising. Instead of reaching for caffeine when I am tired, I can, in less than a minute, do three of the simple techniques (Zip- up, Hook-up, Three Thumps) from Eden's pamphlet for immediate energy—and pass on the caffeine. The exercises are cheaper than caffeine and healthier, as I am energy powered instead of chemically powered.

One more thing to recommend Eden: I was so burned out; my adrenals ached continuously, and it seemed that I never could calm down, even in the nighttime hours. I was in fast motion with only one direction…forward always. My gear was stuck, so to speak. A dear friend advised me to look into my Triple Warmer, as described by Donna Eden. Triple Warmer affects the adrenals, which regulate your fight, flight, and fear responses. I used Donna's techniques to get mine to settle down. It took a few months, but I am much healthier and happier for learning the technique. You may wish to search it out on YouTube.com, her book, or other websites.

Other techniques like Reiki, acupuncture, chiropractic, massage therapists, or the techniques of Barbara Brennan, usually require others to help direct healing to you. You can go online to many of these healing institutions and find a list of licensed or certified healers. Look at credentials, and read reviews. If energy healers do not recognize energy dynamics, instead of helping, they could make body issues worse. This is not a reason to avoid them because great healing can be received if you allow it. These healers can help your energy flow to its optimum level.

In considering both Reiki and Barbara Brennan methods, I encourage you not to shy away from these practices because they seem scary. *Reiki* is a Japanese technique in which a person lays hands on you. The word Reiki is two Japanese words put together; *Rei*, meaning "Gods' wisdom or higher power," and *Ki-*, meaning "life force energy." So *Reiki* means, "Spiritually guided life force energies." I have observed a migraine leave a friend through Reiki. In the light touches of Reiki, you may feel a powerful punch of relief.

The Barbara Brennan method also uses the hands to direct, encourage, and support the body's energies. She teaches more on the paths of the chakras, auric fields, and Hara lines. She is another amazing energy healer who has taught fabulous energy movement techniques. Those trained in her

Reflexology of the Feet
Right Foot

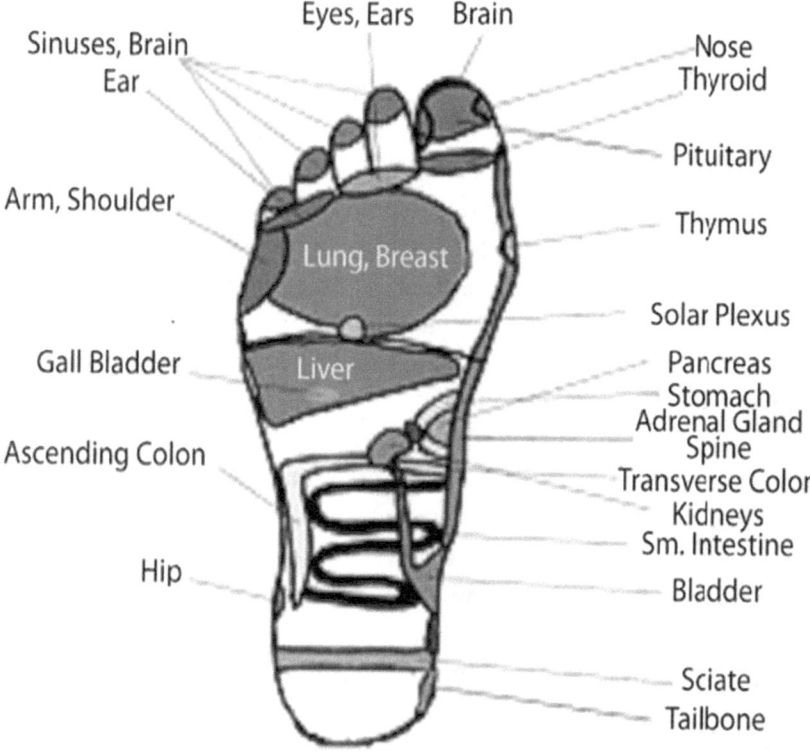

Open Your Heart to the True You

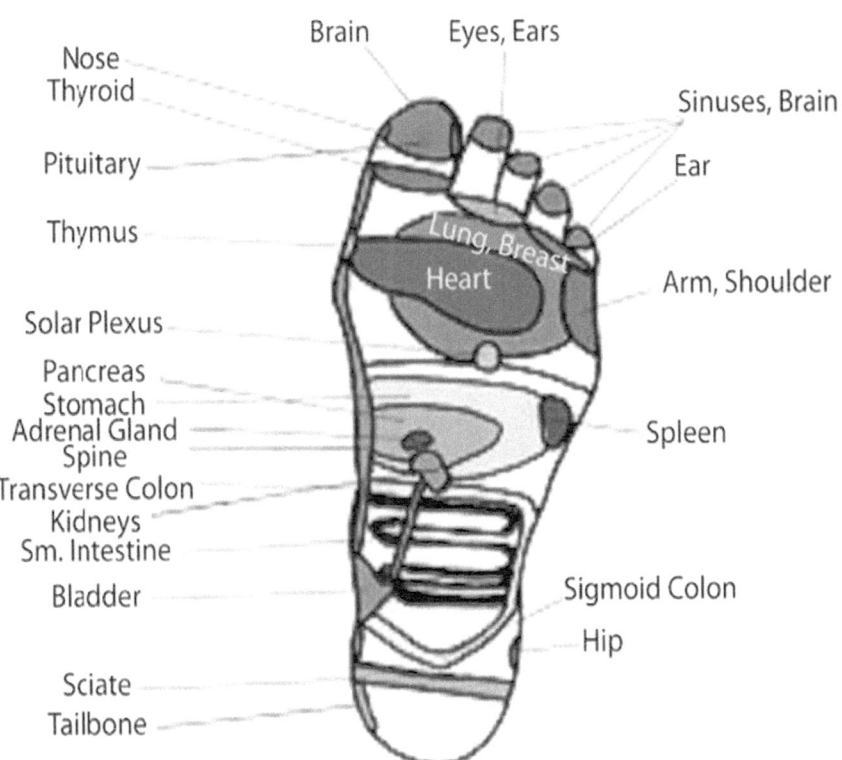

techniques can show you many ways to enhance your own energy flow. One energy pathway she teaches and I find very interesting is the chakra system. She has so many other wonderful energy suggestions that it is beneficial to look over her website, her books *(Hands of Light, Light Emerging)*, and/or locate a certified Brennan method practitioner.

Most people will accept a prayer and being on a prayer list, but they shy away from healers who use touch. These healers need not be looked at as scary. I have wondered why, for so long, Christians have looked down on metaphysical practices such as Reiki, astrology, psychics, energy movement techniques, and other natural and spiritual ways of healing and living. These extraordinary gifts have been given by God, yet many people still believe they are the work of the devil. I find contradictory that Christianity itself follows a doctrine with many miracles, predictions for the future, and healings through touch, but shies away from those ideas today. You may think of Jesus as an example and say, but he was God's perfect son, so of course he could do such things. What about Moses? He parted the Red Sea, turned a staff into a snake, and predicted plagues to Pharaoh. Another example is Elisha. He predicted a barren woman would have a son, and then years later, when the son died, Elisha not only resurrected the son, but healed him. If gifts like these to heal and prophesy were once given to ordinary men, why can't they be given in the current day for the greater good of mankind?

The world we live in now is in need of many miracles, and we are seeing more and more people embrace these more metaphysical paths. They are opening their eyes to see gifts that others would like to share. God is still bestowing gifts today, and many experience wonderful healing touches. God exposes the nasty old secrets many ancient churches told to keep people dependent on churches and priests and away from these practices. Churches wanted to be always required, profitable, and needed, so they taught the only way to survive spiritually was through them. This idea is still being promoted today, knowingly or unknowingly, and sometimes even innocently. When past lies are exposed, we understand energy healings can still be offered to help us grow and heal, both physically and spiritually. Maybe we could start embracing these people into our lives, churches, and hearts for the divine talents they have, for many truly are gifted from God.

You may feel you are not like these healers in having a special gift from God, but there are many gifts that you yourself may give to others. Are you a good cook? Do you have a musical talent? Are you a convincing salesperson? Can you be a true friend to someone? Can you be a wonderful parent today? These are only a few of the talents you may possess. We each have a talent to share, and for the healers mentioned, they will share their talents, if we allow them.

Another area of health that may carry an unfair stigma is mental health. It is hard to have mental health without physical health. It is also hard to have physical health without mental health. Sometimes when we heal the physical body, the mental anguishes heal, too. Other times, by healing the mental turmoil, you can heal the physical body. There is never a set order for obtaining physical and mental health, as healing can happen from either direction, from the mental to the physical or from the physical to the mental. Donna Eden does not analyze the mental concerns of individuals because she feels once the body's energy is flowing, then the mental issues usually work themselves out. Other healers go right to the "How are you?" technique. Sometimes imbedded issues just need a way out, either by talking or by energy movement. A healer of any kind does not give a patient anything the patient does not already have. A healer simply awakens a part of the patient that has been sleeping to the universal healing energies of touch or talk. As you progress, you may eventually outgrow certain healers you have enlisted and move onto others who will help you in other ways. Many good sources exist to give you help as you gain your health. When we realize we are not feeling like we want to feel, then a new need arises in us. This desire to be well leads us to learn and find new ways to get our health back. Here's to good health!

"Energy is eternal delight."
—William Blake

Chakras

We all have chakras, or energy centers, in our bodies. We have seven major chakras and one hundred and twenty-two minor ones; all are linked together. Chakras look like vortexes, disks, wheels, or flower petals that are spinning centers of energy regulating the flow of prana, chi, or Qi throughout your body. The seven major points range from the base of the spine to the top of the head and are connected by a vertical power current. The currents from the major energy points flow through smaller lines of energy called meridians or nadia's, which go into organs and the endocrine system. Even though meridians are also energy systems of lines, chakras are the energy centers along those lines.

These spinning vortexes of energy have different vibrations and colors, and each vortex correlates to a particular section of the body. One of the chakra's many functions is to bring energy to various areas in your body. Another function is to hold the imprint of memory at the chakras, just as memory is held or encoded in your neurons. The chakras are linking mechanisms between the auric fields (energy surrounding a body) and the meridian systems within your body. They also link different levels of the auric fields to the cosmic energy fields. As you can see, they have a big job to do and are very important to each of us.

Every moment chakras give us our energy, but sometimes they do not function as they are meant to. There are many reasons why these centers or the channels between them can get clogged, which in turn do not allow the chakra's (vortexes) to spin or unfold to their full potential, like turning on a fan and then holding the blades so they can't spin. When our chakras are clogged, we become fatigued, sick, or pessimistic. When all energy is connected, spinning to the chakra's optimum frequency happens, and we feel healthy and joyful.

There are many books and web sites about chakras that can provide you with wonderful information. Many certified energy healers can also help you with chakras. Two specific ones are those of Barbara Brennan and Donna Eden. I went to a Barbara Brennan healer and learned a great deal. My solar plexus chakra, which regulates the adrenal gland, was not working optimally, and I was exhausted all the time. I learned that I was used to giving from that particular chakra, but I failed to take energy into it. The healer explained to me that the chakra is like breathing. If all we did was exhale and give, but never inhale and receive, we would die. We need to take in as much as we give out. The healer helped me understand the relationship of the chakras to myself and ways to take energy in, and I felt empowered. These types of healers can also help you!

If you've ever read the book of Revelation from the Bible, you know it is filled with much symbolism of the chakras. Revelation speaks of seven seals, seven churches, seven candlesticks, seven consciousnesses, seven rays, seven bodies, and seven stars. In further study of Revelation, there is much correlation to the seven chakras and seven spiritual centers within Saint John's body and our own. Saint John wrote this book as a first person account of his individual experience and awakening consciousness. No doubt he was experiencing the balance of his seven chakras. Chakras maintain an awareness of our soul's history and can be awakened so we can grow in our awareness.

Chakras tell your story of present and past lives. They can also hold your story back and keep you mired in energy that is stagnant. Our physical, mental, and spiritual evolution are all reflected in the chakras. Clearing and aligning these energies begins to correct the estrangement you may feel from yourself. Balancing the energies can head off an illness and/or heal physical and emotional symptoms. Clearing toxins from today or from long standing issues leaves the body better equipped to heal. Once the energy is unblocked, it can run through you in a cumulative fashion, and your life can unfold according to its intelligent design. Whether our purpose is to raise children, work in a designated field, do research, or help others, our purpose will become evident to us. By finding our purpose, we find our best self and also pass goodness further into the world.

The chakras have every color of the color spectrum, and these colors can be dull or vibrant. The color red is the first and most dense color on the color spectrum, and it is associated with the Root chakra (the 1st one). The colors move up to each chakra in a method resembling the color wheel. It ends at the Crown chakra (7th) with a shade of light purple to white. Each chakra is as unique as a fingerprint and may hold multiple colors within its layers. Chakras can be more complex than some charts show. Each person's chakras are different, just like snowflakes appear similar and yet unique.

There are conflicting descriptions of how the first two chakras are defined. In the first description, the first chakra is called the Root chakra, and it relates to the solids of you—your bones, all things rooted in you, survival, and the things that keep you grounded. This definition also includes the sexual organs, since they too are a grounding force and procreation is needed to sustain humanity and guarantee the survival of the human race. That leaves the second chakra (Womb or Sacral) as the "creative endeavors chakra," which includes not only pregnancy—growing that human for the next nine months—but all the other creative endeavors you may have throughout your lifetime, including creative ways of having intercourse.

The second description describes the second chakra (Womb or Sacral) as not just creativity, but also as procreation. The first chakra is only for the solids of you and nothing more. These two differing descriptions help you understand that there will be individual interpretations in chakras. Some cultures only count six chakras instead of seven, as they combine both the first and second chakras into one. There will be differences of opinion regarding chakras from continent to continent and from person to person. You may choose not to get muddled in all the differences and just learn of ways to bring about your health without labels attached.

Here is a quick rundown of my own interpretation of chakras from the many books I have read:

Root Chakra – 1-Red: Survival and sexuality. Carries your life force down legs for support. Here is your grounding in earth and your primordial life force. Self-survival and sexual urges since producing children is a life force for humanity's survival.

Sacral/Womb Chakra – **2-Orange:** Your right brain activity and your growth of initial endeavors. Our female energy is here. Babies grow, projects germinate, and creativity flourishes. You assimilate and eliminate food since food causes your growth and digestive organs are here. Chakra 2 is the essential "me" place of creativity. It embraces your soul. This chakra is by the navel, which not only held the umbilical cord attached to your mother, but is also your own energetic connection to the pure creative energy still nourishing you. We must all continue to have a passion and a creative plug in.

Solar Chakra – **3-Yellow:** Here is our left-brain activity, identity and power; where we discriminate and are assertive. Here is our male energy. This is where parental and social messages are encoded.

Heart Chakra – **4-Green:** Here is love and compassion. Love rules rather than logic; it's your heart over your head. Chakra 4 needs balance as one can love too much. Love is unconditional here in a healthy chakra; it gives love to self and to others.

Throat Chakra – **5-Shades of blue/turquoise:** Our verbal expression is here. The throat is known as the Holy Grail, since it bridges much knowledge and links the lower chakras (1-4), which are related to our physical aspects, to the higher chakras (6 & 7), which are ether aspects. Energy in both directions merges into speech here. In this chakra, you may either have trouble speaking up or shutting up. This Chakra can have too much energy or not enough energy based on how the thyroid and hyoid bone are regulated.

Third Eye Chakra – **6-Deep blue or indigo:** Here is deep perception and understanding. We receive guidance that transcends our usual knowing. This guidance can be dominated by too much thought or mental turbulence, so it needs to be grounded with the lower chakras (1-4), which are more subtle ways of knowing and being.

Crown Chakra – **7-Shades of purple or almost white:** Our transcendence of self is here. We are at one with the universe and have deep peace and comprehension. Meditation, prayer, and chakra opening are ways to strengthen this transcendence.

***

A lower chakra does not mean a less spiritual chakra. Sometimes dropping lower/deeper into the lower chakras is greatly needed. The lower chakras have as much spiritual significance as the higher ones. In a game of football, you can hold the ball in your hands, but unless you are grounded with your feet to the ground, you won't be able to run the ball and have a game. You could only have a mental game without any physical action. Or, if you have the grounded feet running but don't have the football to play with, the game would only be running. This is why all the chakras need to be hooked up equally without any one being viewed as dominant or weak. The game of life becomes so much easier, healthier, and fun!

An external energy called feng shui is popular today. The energy of cluttered belongings can block or slow us down mentally, emotionally, physically, and even spiritually. The clutter, or position of material objects in your home, office, purse, and vehicle, can truly affect your energy, or chi. This will in turn affect your health, finances, relationships, and many other little things in your life. As hair in a shower or tub drain can clog the flow of water, clogged energy internally and externally can also slow our energy flow. A wonderful book on this subject is *Clearing the Clutter for Good Feng Shui*, by Mary Lambert.

The energy of the auric field or aura is part of our energy system that penetrates the body and extends beyond the body. The first layer of energy is very close to our body and all other multiple layers expand outward. It can be referred to as the etheric body, energetic double, or sphere of energy, and it serves as a filter or antenna protecting you from negative energy and pulling in positive energy. If you are sick, your aura can collapse in on you to protect yourself and your organs. If you are in good health, the aura will expand greatly. Aura is an energy that surrounds all matter, and all matter has an atomic structure that gives off energy. A human being has layers of physical, emotional, mental, and spiritual elements. Auras contain all the primary colors of the rainbow at any given time and change color depending on the emotion an individual is experiencing. Happy and loving thoughts will also expand the aura, while sad or angry thoughts will contract the energy. Energy comes from within and also from outside us. The chakras help pull both the external and internal energy in and throughout our bodies.

When you think of your own body as a major power plant, you see a truly amazing factory, a factory that should be given our respect and attention. A good flowing energy system helps us reach our potential. Learning about our chakra system and clearing out the physical clutter around us will free up these energy vortexes and energy fields. I looked up one day and saw a rainbow with such defined and distinct colors. Have you ever seen one of those rainbows? It dawned on me the rainbow was the exact color order of the chakra color order in our own bodies. Our planet has its very own energy system, too. Look up and appreciate the rainbow in the sky as you appreciate the rainbow in you.

I have included a chart to help distinguish the chakras. Remember, ideas about the general description of each chakra can vary in Eastern and Western cultures.

Chakra Locations

Chart of the Chakras and Their Descriptions

Chakra	Root	Sacral/Womb	Solar
Color	Red	Orange	Yellow
Symbol	Square w/ triangle facing downward	Crescent	Downward pointing red triangle
Note	Do	Re	Mi
Vibration	4	6	10
Sanskrit Name	Muldhara	Svadhisthana	Manipura
Planet Assoc.	Mars	Sun	Mercury
Element	Earth	Water	Fire
Association	Smell	Taste	Sight
Assoc. Body Part	Teeth and Bones	Fluids in Body, Carries Oxygen	Adrenals
Description	Grounding Force to Earth Energy/ Sexual	Creative Expression/ Gestation	Self Esteem & Personality

Continued

Heart	Throat	Brow	Crown
Green	Sky Blue	Indigo Blue	Purple
Hexagram (two overlapping triangles)	Circle inside downward pointing triangle	Downward pointing golden triangle	Lotus Flower w/open petals
Fa	So	La	Ti
12	16	96	968
Anahata	Vissuda	Anja	Sahasrara
Saturn	Jupiter	Venus	Moon
Air			
Touch	Ether	Ether	Ether
Heart, Lung, Thymus, Endocrine	Thyroid and Endocrine	Pituitary, Pineal, & Eyes	Pineal Gland, Endocrine
Unconditional Love of Self & Others	Communication & Truth	Intuition/ A Higher Knowing	One with Universe

*"I make myself rich by making
my needs and wants few."*
—Henry David Thoreau

Simplify

Perhaps you've heard, "The simpler we become, the closer to God we get," and as we get closer to God, we get closer to our very selves. By simplifying, in all areas, we make our lives effortless. The word *simplify* can be applied to so many things—the clutter in our homes or offices, cars or trucks, wallets or purses. Even the way we schedule our calendars and think can be cluttered! By simplifying mentally and physically, we have less clutter to hold onto, and all aspects of our lives will become easier.

Have you ever gone on a trip or vacation and been amazed at the small number of items you pack? You take what is important to you or what you think will be needed. Whether in a condo, a hotel room, or a house, haven't you felt freer because of the lack of clutter in your temporary living space? Sometimes on those trips, you get a glimpse of what really matters and how the bare-bones of the surroundings bring a sense of tranquility. Then you go home to your house where you have spent years accumulating and storing. It is bursting at the seams with gadgets, collections, keepsakes, and photographs, and you think, why do I have all this stuff? Sometimes trips on which you've taken a minimum amount of "stuff," or visiting a home of simplicity, makes you realize how much you have acquired. I like to clean out, but sometimes I lose track of my recent accumulations, and I need those little reminders to get me motivated to once again inventory my stuff. I liken it to our children growing. You are with them all the time and do not see how much they grew because it is in small increments. One day you realize their pants are two inches too short or they can't get their feet into their shoes. How many of us slowly acquire more without even realizing what we've acquired? I love those "ah-ha" or "ouch" moments to help me again see the stuff that has slowly crept in on me. Seeing serenity in uncluttered surroundings is that kind of "ah-ha" moment to me, and then I want to go home and work on my stuff again. Those moments of realization help me remember what truly matters in my life, like family, friends, and simplicity. Remember, you can still instill your own style with the "less is more" approach. It is simplifying and being who you truly are, at its best.

When you think of "spring cleaning", you think of freshening things up and dusting them off. When you think of "simplify cleaning," you think of not having to clean, dust off, freshen up, or wearisomely shuffle around because you don't have the stuff in the first place. "Simplify cleaning" is the initial work of purging excess or unused stuff, so you can later do maintenance or spring cleaning. It is okay to have things because we are here to enjoy that part of physicality here on earth, too. Contrary to what some say, we can be very enlightened and spiritual even with our material possessions. It is only when we feel overwhelmed or burdened by them that the balance needs restored. That is when the simplifying should be initiated. Have fun with it, and see if you start to breathe easier with each organizing step you take.

I started in my basement. I asked myself if I still had emotional attachment to certain items. If I felt I could live without it and without regret of giving it away, then I simplified my life. Sometimes our attachments to items are amazing because the items and our attachment to them begin to define who we are. What would happen if that perceived safety net of attachments were taken away? Could you still be who you are without the stuff to shuffle, store, and dust? I compare it to wearing makeup. Cosmetics makes us feel pretty and fresh, but can you go to the store without your makeup or does makeup define who you are to the point you can't leave home without it? Wearing makeup is fine, but when we define ourselves by it, we are out of balance. When we internalize who we are by our possessions, again, we are out of balance. Only you know what individual possessions mean to you. Only you know how much work or practice you need on your balance beam. I went through my stuff keeping this in mind. Sometimes I wasn't sure, so I held that group of stuff in a different area until I knew. The other stuff went to the "keep group" or the "give-away" pile. When I'd gone through everything, I organized my keep group.

After starting small in my basement, I moved to junk drawers and closets. If I hadn't worn an item in a while, I seriously looked at it. Did it still fit? If it did, I tried it on and decided if I still wanted to wear it. I analyzed even the jeans in the bottom of the closet because maybe I really didn't like the cut or the color. How many socks can one person really wear? How many t-shirts and shoes do you want to have as space-keepers or decorations? How many cookbooks can a person use? I cleaned out those, too. If you only have a few favorite recipes in a book, copy them and put them in a recipe folder or a three-ring binder. The same can be done with all those magazines no one ever seems to get rid of. If you're saving the magazines for only an article or two, tear those articles out, label them, and put them in a three-ring binder. How about men who keep every nail, bolt, screw, electrical wire, duplicate tools or wrenches, just in case? My wise husband once asked me, "How much can you bring into the house without taking stuff out of the house?" Where do you put all your stuff? Do you need to rent a storage unit to house your stuff?

I stopped buying at good sales if I was only going to store and save my purchases for a possibility—say, a future birthday party my kids might get invited to. I cleaned out stacks of papers that had been lying around for years. I couldn't believe what was buried in those stacks! What had I been thinking?

We change, and when we do, the stuff we enjoyed at one time may not be anything we can relate to anymore. I've read that every seven years, a person changes significantly. Have you ever heard that? Think of what you've collected, thought, or navigated to over the last seven years. How about twenty years back? Are you still that same person? Our values, preferences, and personalities change. We assume we will always be exactly the same with only a few more wrinkles, but this illusion is why many get ill-advised tattoos, make bad financial deals, or hang onto personal belongings.

I started to recycle by giving to other people if they wanted my burden as their treasure. We've all heard "One man's trash is another man's treasure," and this form of recycling felt really nice and was also liberating. However, there is also the saying, "If it is junk, then your junk may still be another man's junk, and it may just need tossed." Use common sense. Go through cupboards and throw away expired goods. Another thought is not give expired goods to food drives. Pay attention to their expiration date. That is a no-brainer. But, carry over that expiration date philosophy to other items, and ask what has expired in your closets, medicine chests, drawers, purse, and so on, and throw away expired goods and foods, or recycle it according to your county or state recycling laws.

I think back on how my grandparents held onto what seemed like everything they came across. They lived through the Depression, and both remembered sometimes having no food or extras. They saved every scrap of fabric, every button, every twist-tie. They saved shoes with holes, just in case the ones they were wearing got even worse than the holey ones they'd saved. Anytime a canned item was on sale, it found a home in their pantry, and eventually, some of the cans got so old, they exploded. I don't know the mental unease my grandparents felt going through those hard times, but it must have been great. Most of us, though, have not lived through a Great Depression. All I am saying is, if you can move things out and around your home to enhance your well-being and comfort, give it a try. Once the initial work is done, it will be so much easier to keep up with later. Simplifying will then become just spring cleaning.

Another way to simplify our lives is to look at holiday preparations. Now, if you truly get joy from decorating, then this section doesn't apply to you. If, however, you feel burdened by the mere thought of approaching holidays, your holiday preparations need to be simplified.

I used to go to extremes on Thanksgiving and Christmas. Those are still fun and special holidays for me, but there was a time I turned the enjoyment of my extremes into my personal drudgery. This past year, I gave away one-third of my holiday decorations. Then, I only put half of what was left out for the holidays. I did less baking, and in essence, later had less weight to work off. I thought back on holidays my father-in-law said were special to him, those when he got an orange in his stocking. We have come so far away from that simple ideal! Do you have a "gifts to buy" list that has no end? Holidays are to be special and filled with love. How can they be love when they are filled with stress and drudgery? If all the holiday preparations are becoming a burden to you, look at what you're doing and simplify.

Years ago, I laughed at George Carlin's skit about other people's stuff. Carlin made light of people renting little homes or storage units to house all the stuff that didn't fit into the house they already lived in. I thought it funny at the time, but I realize it is a growing and still perplexing issue today. What do we do with our "extra" stuff? So many new storage unit buildings are springing up everywhere, and while this is surely making the owners of storage unit's wallets thicker, it is making the renters' wallets thinner. You have to sincerely ask, is having the stuff worth the financial or mental investment? I am intrigued and left wondering why so many are attached to so much stuff. They save most things, gaze upon them or feel secure just knowing they are in a box or storage unit close by. Why and what is happening in our lives that so much is needed? This kind of acquisition isn't true fulfillment; it is only masquerading as fulfillment.

I want to clarify that I in no way judge anyone who wishes to enjoy his accumulations. I would never come into your home and judge your stuff, either lack of or excess of. You have the choice to live as you wish; that is what diversity is. My point is we each, individually, need to ask ourselves, "Do we own our stuff or does our stuff own us?" When possessions are dragging you down in body, mind, and soul, then your stuff and your thoughts need to be simplified.

We can also simplify the drama in our lives. Drama may have served us through a piece of our lives, but there comes a point when one no longer needs it. Is it time to simplify the situations in your life? Are you a person who enjoys all the fuss and pretentious gossip that precedes and follows all details of your living or are you a person who is tired by and of it? If emotional complications are wearing you down, try to see how much of drama you can drop from your life, either by eliminating problematic situations from your own speech and actions or by walking away from others' thorny issues. We know there is a lot of drama in the world. Notice the grocery check-out aisles and the many magazines catering to drama frenzy. Do you really care how a celebrity died or why a person you've never met left his partner? At work, does it really matter how a co-worker got a luxurious vacation or expensive piece of jewelry? Does the water cooler talk refresh you or make you feel burdened and judgmental? Would you be more refreshed through simplification by elimination there, too?

One more aspect of simplifying: Are you still holding on to a lot of the past? How much of it do you still need? Have those events passed their expiration dates? Are you tired of dusting "what could have been?" off and moving it around in your head? Can you free up some space to move around and breathe to make space for today? Whether your possessions are material or psychological, do they own you or do you own them? Simplifying in every area of your life: Simplify, simplify, simplify. Refresh, refresh, refresh.

*"Putting a foot down is a prerequisite
for stepping ahead."*
—Alan Cohen

Busy Overload

Are you too busy? Are you feeling buried with multiple to-dos or to-go-tos? Face it, most of us are experiencing "busy overload." How many of us could cut down on some of the busy-ness, if we tried? Schedules need to be regularly critiqued, and depending on the season of your life, critiquing may need to be done more frequently to assure balance. Many of us don't realize how busy we have become until the busy-ness is out of proportion with what our bodies can handle. We get beaten down by daily living; we are pushed to do more, to produce more, to make more money, or to be more perfect in ourselves. Either we guilt ourselves or let others guilt us into taking on more than we desire. With all the "more, more, more," we neglect our body, mind, and spirit, and even though this busy-ness takes its toll and leaves us exhausted, we do it over and over again. Sometimes we need to shelter ourselves from the rest of the world and take care of ourselves so we don't suffer later. We all need to be nurtured, and we need space and time in which to nurture ourselves; finding that space and time may mean turning down the volume of chaos.

Have you ever heard the phrase "spread too thin"? I pondered where this phrase originated, and how it applied in life. Was it coined referring to food spread on a piece of bread and how spreading the food too thinly would not give much nutrition to the end product? Did it refer to spreading something like bread dough that rips or tears when rolled out too far? If we physically or mentally spread ourselves too thin, we are being unkind to our body and mind. Have you ever noticed how a stressed person will start to gain weight? Your body acknowledges you are stressed, and your metabolism slows down so healing can occur when food is given. You may feel more tired, too because your body wants you to rest and heal from the stress you're experiencing. Stress is stress, no matter what category you place it in, and your body will deal with that stress as it was designed to. It does not distinguish between hunger and too many board meetings. Illness, because of stress, provides information about the fit between your body's needs and your lifestyle. When being too suddenly stretched to extremes, you can experience illness or fatigue. When you ignore your body's demand to slow down, it will find a way to make you slow down. Your mind may follow artificial rhythms like clocks and calendars, but your internal body follows the natural rhythms of its own internal clock and the rhythm of the planets in heaven. You will not be able to trick a natural rhythm for long. Instead of fighting your body's rhythm, try to stay in alignment with it.

There are a host of difficulties that can arise from the high cortisol levels caused by stress. Not only does stress give you the belly fat, but can also cause faster aging of the physical body and the breakdown of nerve cells in the brain. Too much cortisol caused by stressors, over long periods of time, results in the breakdown of structural tissues in muscle, bone, skin, and the brain, all of which ages a person prematurely. Stress severely changes your sleep patterns; often you can't get to sleep or stay asleep, or you wake up too early. Stress affects absorption of food, minerals, and hormones (thyroid, insulin, testosterone, estrogen, progesterone, melatonin, and serotonin). The gut, adrenals, and kidneys are also severely affected. If that doesn't give a person reason to slow down, I don't know what will! Our goal should be learning and working at ways to be kind to our body by finding ways to decrease some of our stress.

Do you make yourself too readily available to others? I grew up in a life style of always giving because giving was Christ-like, but there was also a flip side that I failed to see until much later in my life. The flip side is that even Christ made plenty of quiet time for himself. There are several places in the Bible that refer to him retreating or reclining. After I got married, my husband was the first to point out my unbalanced giving. I was always readily available to take every phone call or request from my friends and family, even while I was having a meal. Maybe I liked the drama or didn't know how to say no, but he helped me see that calls and other activities could wait until I had had time to nourish myself. Are you also too available and not taking time to nourish yourself? Can you sit down and have a meal on your own or with your family?

Nowadays, you don't physically have to talk with your mouth full since phones have texting capabilities. Communicating can be done by only using our fingers and the same concept of always being available is not only present, but heightened. Now we can talk and text at the same time! Is there a way to decrease your use of texting, instant messaging, Facebook, internet searching, and emailing? While there is nothing wrong with these marvels of design, they can easily be overused. I don't deny the convenience or safety of being "connected": your kids or your partner can give you a quick text or IM to announce they are in, or need to be picked up, or have to stay after school for practice. But phones are used for so much more. People try to carry on a conversation with a physical person in a room while conversing over numerous texts with a cyber-person. How many executives have you seen in meetings who text during the meeting? I was at lunch the other day, and out of five occupied tables, three tables had all patrons texting through lunch. It was very interesting to watch. A head occasionally looked up and interjected a comment, as if to say, "Yes I am still here," and then the head quickly went back to the electronic device in its hand. Were these people practicing multitasking at its best or simply avoiding those next to them?

I am amused by the realization the handler is being abused by an electronic device. We humans do not realize how enraptured we have become with multi-tasking and multiple stimuli. Continual multi-tasking is not generally the healthiest approach to life. I thought the other day about how years ago, when you saw someone with a cell phone, you thought, he must be really important since he needs to be on call all the time. Now, in the present day, when I see people on cell phones I think, they must be really stupid to have to be available all the time. Times sure have changed. I also remember times when we recognized behaviors as rude and thoughtless that we now just accept, like using cell phones in check-out lines and elevators or in places of interacting with your family; phoning or texting while driving; talking loudly and inappropriately in public, so others are pulled into your conversation; sending pictures or messages electronically that should never be out in internet space for anyone to retrieve; and forgetting how to have a face-to-face or look-you-in-the eye social interaction.

If you find yourself burdened by being always connected and the desire to answer and be too available is unbearable, the answer is simple: those devices may just need to be turned off or left in the pocket. Common courtesy would stop us from offering a recovering alcoholic an alcoholic drink. Common sense would stop us from shopping for fun if we don't have money. How does your common sense guide you in handling your electronic devices? If you have to decrease the temptation, turn off the devices and leave them home for awhile. Show those physical bodies around you they are important. Show yourself you are important, important enough to have time to yourself.

You may convince yourself you just have to answer that one more text, message, or phone call so you can get it done and out of the way, but friends, here is the absolute truth. "It" will never be done. You can never get "it" all done. There will always be "just one more." Life is always a to-do list. When we finish that to-do list, life is over. You don't want to get "it" done! Place things in pause mode and enjoy your meal, your conversation with the friend who is physically present, or a quiet reflective moment on your own. People will eventually accept the fact that you will not be available every second of the day for all those beck and calls. You have a life that is not solely attached to electronics or to them. People have survived for many years without electronics, and I am not advocating going totally without them. I am encouraging you to turn them off for a little much needed down-time.

Is your life too attached to others' to-do lists? Do you help others when, really, your own soul needs attention? How many times do you say, "Yes," when you know you should've said, "No"? How many times have you kicked yourself later for something you really shouldn't have taken on? We humans speak many languages fluently, but the word "no" is not spoken enough in any language. You can tell others you are scheduled somewhere else without lying if you physically pen yourself in on your calendar for that "me" time. Sometimes actually seeing our own name written on the calendar encourages you to follow through with that appointment to yourself. Respect yourself by making spaces of time for you and your needs.

A good place to start is to cut out some volunteer work. Volunteer first to yourself until you feel refreshed. If you are still sad about not doing community involvement work, you can put your gloves on, get garbage bags, go out into your neighborhood or park, and pick up trash at your own designated time. You can help the earth and do walking meditation while performing community service. Also, you can ask your partner for help with some of the home and family burdens if your partner isn't also overloaded. Maybe the two of you can split the duties and/or let some unimportant things go around the house. Can your children do more around the house, too?

As you make yourself a priority, you teach your family to make themselves a priority too, If your kids are overscheduled with too many extra clubs, sports, or extracurricular activities, maybe they too are feeling overloaded and are waiting for someone to step in and teach them ways of carving out down-time! You and your family cannot constantly give and not refill your tanks. As we said before, it's like breathing. What would happen if all you did was exhale without ever inhaling? Find time to nourish your souls. Try to quiet your world in all ways, so you have some moments of "quiet think." Remember, when we have quiet, we can hear our higher selves. If we always have the music up loud, the television on, or to-dos going on, we may not hear what we should hear.

The metaphysical community (metaphysical—that which is beyond physical awareness), says we are in an amazing evolutionary time at present, and we can, individually, move into our own heightened and sped up evolution. We can grow in leaps and bounds in these upcoming years. Who of us does not want to evolve into a better person? Technology has done us all many favors in making our lives easier. We no longer have to take a horse to town or do laundry outside in a tub basin. When we think of technology as a positive force, we can do much for ourselves by giving ourselves quiet, uncluttered, un-busy time to continue evolving.

Once you've made time for yourself and your family, you can get out into nature. Nature gives you a grounded presence and rejuvenates your energy; being in nature makes you want to slow down. Try sitting in the shade under a tree pondering; sit in the sun and soak up the rays, or sit on a porch and look up and out into the beautiful horizon. Watch and listen to a steady rain, and let your mind be calm. Sit in a rocking chair and be the rhythm of the rock! How about sitting and reading a book you have longed to read? Have you wanted to explore with your camera? Is there a musical instrument you've been longing to try? Is there a picture you wanted to draw? A meditation practice you wanted to try? When did you last have time to nap uninterrupted? How about walking among your flowers and really smelling them or touching the leaves and bark of a tree? Walk barefoot in the soft grass. Walk in newly fallen snow and feel it crunch under your boots. Try enjoying the simplicity of snow's beautiful covering telling you there is still simplicity and ease in you and your world. How about taking a nice leisurely walk in the early morning newness or a warm bath calling you for a soak as the day draws to a close? Am I getting you excited about having a few carefree and easy minutes for yourself? Go ahead. Put yourself in "me-time" or schedule yourself in. Don't put off till tomorrow what you may need today.

There is a part in the animated cartoon, *Winnie the Pooh's Grand Adventure*, that references to doing nothing as just listening and not bothering. I love that part of the movie because I have a hard time just doing nothing. Even meditation has me itching to move and do something. I believe there are probably many more people like me. Can we learn together to do a little more of "nothing"?

Working to decrease your busyness overload may not be easy at first or even doable at times, but even a few changes will offer you a break to de-stress. You and your family may want to start slow. If you cut out many things all at once, you may not feel comfortable with the new quiet, and your discomfort could propel you, out of habit, back into hectic scenarios. Going into easy mode can feel like spinning your wheels or like your foot is at the starting line with no race to run. When I first started to cut out busyness, it felt odd, like the first few days of a vacation when I try to adjust into easy mode. Just like vacation, you can enjoy the benefits of occasionally quieting your home, life, and mind from over-load and the physical and mental noise pollution of too much communication.

We all long for that soft armchair. Not that you really need a soft armchair to slow down, but sitting in one just may work its magic in taking you towards that goal. That armchair mode will get us to the flip-side of our serving personalities. We all need the serving and the savoring to really be healthy. We can find ways to ease into a relaxing life for today, tomorrow, or a lifetime.

*"Mother Nature gives us much from her plate. We are always invited as her guest,
if we want to be."*
—Renee Salvatori

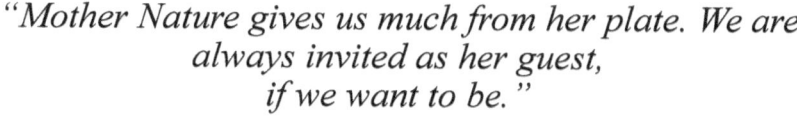

Essences from Nature

Essences are made from minuscule amounts of substances from plants: seeds, bark, leaves, stem, roots, flowers, or fruit. Homeopathy, essential oils, herbs, and flower essences all use different parts and different dilutions (sometimes as dilute as one part per ten billion) of the plant being used. The use of the essence determines which part of and to what degree the plant will be processed. Many plants have been used safely throughout millennia. Essences have been identified in Egyptian hieroglyphics and ancient Chinese manuscripts. Even the Bible references essences a hundred and eighty-eight times; remember frankincense, myrrh, and rosemary? Native American Indians had amazing success using plants medicinally and passed on this art to others who arrived in the new world. Today, this art form is once again being appreciated as people look for alternative healing methods.

Think of how people use candles, air fresheners, and perfumes, and you will understand using a similar approach to essential oils. However, essential oils are very pure, and you should always purchase the purest oils you can, as this assures purity of the product and your safety. Pure essential oils are usually used *externally* and can also be placed into a diffuser to dispense into the air around you for a pure form of aromatic enjoyment, like smelling a flower. A couple of my favorite essences are lavender as it is calming, rose fills me with love, and orange boost the immune system. Young Life and DoTerra are a couple of the brands I have used. If you investigate essences, make sure you understand and learn which products can be taken internally and which should only be used externally.

Disease is usually a result of deep and long acting forces from within. *Allopathic* medicine is the treatment of disease by using remedies whose effects differ from those produced by that disease and may help the surface issues. *Homeopathic* medicine is a complimentary treatment which a patient is given minute doses of natural substances that produce the same symptoms of the disease itself and heals at a different level. Homeopathic has the ability to go to the root cause. Both are safe for humans and animals.

There is evidence that in the years of the Black Death, people were able to survive using a specific mixture of lemon, cinnamon, clove, rosemary, and eucalyptus. In the Homeopathic community, this is known as The Five Thieves Remedy. Today, it can be purchased already made up or you can make your own according to a formula.

Essences are an investment. If you do not have funds for many different remedies, start with two of my favorites: Rescue Remedy and Sleep Remedy from Bach Flower Essences. These products are so safe even babies can take them. The Bach brand is also safe for those with gluten allergies. The alcohol used to preserve the essences (a very small amount) is made from grapes and is gluten-free. Another brand, Nelson's, uses cane sugar alcohol as its preservative, and it, too, is gluten-free. Have you noticed you can now purchase homeopathic teething tablets and colic water at regular drug and grocery stores? These remedies tend to be much safer for the liver than allopathic acetaminophen and gas tablets. As more and more people are beginning to understand this new healing world, more premade remedies can be purchased at grocery stores, health stores, and online.

 My favorite company for essences is Bach Flower Essences, mentioned above. They offer quick help for your mental and/or emotional outlook without needing a great deal of time to research; the research has already been done. These medications can be psychotherapy in a bottle for situations like divorce or surgery. Their ability to relieve stress, anxiety, and tension is tremendous, and these remedies have helped me more times than I can count. Other remedies in the homeopathic line, which you may need to research and study, not only help your emotional side, but also your physical side. They can treat conditions like broken bones, poison ivy, and various infections. A good source to purchase these pure types of homeopathic remedies is www.

archeusonline.com. Researching homeopathy and oils will start you into a different world of healing.

Nature has given us so much from her plate. We eat the obvious produce yet do not partake of the equally beneficial but less obvious. We spray our yards to kill weeds like dandelions and stinging nettles and we think we have beautiful yards, but our internal landscapes are not so good looking, and those "weeds" we kill off could help. If you researched how beneficial eating dandelion greens are, you might start welcoming that little plant. Grocery stores now carry fresh dandelion leaves and teas. When my mother-in-law was younger, she ate train loads of dandelions. Her family was always searching for them. They would sauté dandelions, add them as flavoring to other dishes, or eat them raw as a salad. After she married, she still made dandelion salads whenever she had dandelions available. She is now in her nineties!

Essences from nature can seem like a different world, but once you begin to explore and understand, even a little bit, the world of essences quickly begins to make sense. The trial and error research of time has already been completed on these remedies; all we need to do is read the recommendations. When we trust that Nature is not holding any secrets from us, we can certainly enjoy all her bounty.

"Every artist was first an amateur."
—Ralph Waldo Emerson

Find a Creative Outlet

Creativity is such a vital element to our health, but how many of us go through life without having any outlet of creativity? Those poor souls suffer from artistic constipation. When we have an inventive or artistic desire, we feel alive and look forward to living. When we stifle this desire, we feel weighed down and unwell. To be alive and healthy, we must continue to have desires, fantasies, and dreams to fan our creative fires. What is a creative outlet for you? Pick an *artistic* or *athletic* endeavor where you can express and be yourself. The possibilities are literally endless.

Creativity is not just painting or drawing. It includes so many other things. Cooking, biking, dancing (slow, jazz, belly dance, video game dancing, square or folk dance, or just swaying with any song), singing (in the shower or car, if not in public), golfing (putt-putt or regular), scrapbooking, drawing (on a napkin, on a canvas, or in a sketch book), coloring (mandalas or coloring books), gardening (pots inside or planting outside), jogging, pottery, music of any kind (listening or playing; there are even little package drums sets that teach you to use the drum beats to connect to yourself), needlework, quilting, crocheting or knitting, cycling (bicycle or motorcycle), bird watching, bowling, acting, origami, paper twirling art, wood carving, whittling (wood, soap, wax, or stone), painting (by numbers or on a canvas; with watercolor, oils, or pastels), sculpting (clay, Play-Doh, or other mediums), writing (journals, music, poetry, or books), reading (fiction or non-fiction), sports of all kinds, studies of something, chess, or photography? You choose!

My family still laughs at my dance moves when I express my creative outlet; it serves as free entertainment for them. Laughing is an outlet too, right? Your family, like mine, may wonder what you are up to at first, but they will respect you soon enough for recognizing and giving yourself your own expression. They may even start some of their own personal expressions of creativity (which may serve to entertain you).

Try not to tell yourself, "I can't do this!" because you are only boxing yourself in. Vincent Van Gogh said, "If you hear a voice within you say, 'you cannot paint' then by all means paint, and that voice will be silenced." We don't have to be good at anything to do it. Remember the saying that the Titanic was built by professionals, but the ark was built by amateurs? There is only one thing you need, and that is excitement. You don't need to be an expert! It doesn't matter if you have a canvas to work with or a paper napkin. When you have the desire to create, the desire will find its way out. Be creative and see how good it can feel.

We are all a spark of God and thus have creating abilities in us. We are all familiar with how God, as recounted in the book of Genesis, created the heavens and earth, day and night, animals on land and creatures in the sea. On the first day God created...and so the story goes through the seventh day. A day to God is like a thousand years, so it appears God took His time creating this art form and enjoyed it. God didn't create everything in one day. We, too, can spread out our creations and endeavors. Creating is an art form that will reflect all your thoughts, whatever your age. One season in your life may reflect a different creative outlet than another season. Your age, personality, and life style can all affect the endeavors you enjoy.

In the book of Genesis 1:31 it says, "Then God saw everything that was made, and indeed IT WAS very good." So be God-like: get motivated enough to find something you can create and feel excited about. Pablo Picasso was referring to his artistic endeavors when he said, "Action is the foundational key to all success." Success for Picasso did not refer to the money he made from his creations, but to the feeling of accomplishment he had from making them. Anytime we accomplish something, we have a feeling of success. Can you think of a time you felt that powerful feeling of accomplishment and satisfaction? What you create in the future may only be for you, but nonetheless, it feels so good to be the creator of something! That something you create also propels you into a more grounded presence here on earth. You are expanding the physical part of you, by using your hands, body, and mind in expression. You are placing roots here. You are, in essence, saying, "I am here!" Your creativity is monumental to who you are because creativity is a further expression of who you truly are.

> *"The ease of health comes first through the ease of thought."*
> —Renee Salvatori

Health and Other Snippets

Health suggestions come to us today as if offered from a buffet table. When we stand at a real buffet table, we choose what food or condiments appeal to us or work well for us. We must do the same with suggestions about our health. Enjoy the many choices available and have fun with the different ideas to which you are introduced, for many of you the buffet table's health suggestions will enhance your health or recuperation in the long run.

If you need a physical, please see a doctor. Do understand there will be times when no amount of meditating or mirror work helps, and a thorough physical may be needed. You can use both allopathic and/or homeopathic doctors' recommendations; the two are not mutually exclusive. Illnesses and other emotional discomforts provide useful information about the fit between the body's needs and life style. Finding the right fit for your body is like trying on different outfits or different shoes. You try on several styles of clothing, you look in the mirror to check them out, and you move around a little to make sure each style will function well on you. You must do the same with health and other enlightening ideas and activities you try in your life. Once you find that good fit, you will begin healing in many ways, whether through a medical approach or through simple lifestyle alterations.

When a person is young, the illness created from his lifestyle of neglect may not show up immediately. After years upon years of not making healthy eating and drinking choices, living in a polluted household or environment, not getting physical exercise, and experiencing the common mental and physical stresses of day to day life, the body will experience a cumulative effect that may later manifest itself as mental or physical illness. This person may look into his recent past and wonder how he got to this point, but sometimes his illnesses may have started years in the past. Whether the illness or issue is from something he did yesterday or a decade ago, the illness or issue is asking for attention when it shows up. The more a person engages in healing his body, the more health will come to him. Like a crystal prism, healing will draw more and more healing in and around itself. He will begin not only to receive healing and health, but to give healing and health to others.

After many years of sicknesses, my medical doctor determined I was very anemic, had many food allergies, had out of sync hormones, and was generally stressed. My many issues heaped each on top of the other for years before finally getting my attention. My doctor gave me answers, so I could begin to understand what I needed to change.

A saliva hormone test revealed I was severely lacking in two hormones, so my doctor prescribed the exact hormones I needed as supplements, and years of panic attacks and sleep deprivation disappeared virtually overnight. My monthly cycles eased up, and thus my anemia got better. If you even slightly suspect your hormones are out of balance, get them checked, preferably with a saliva test as evidence shows the results may be more reliable than those from a blood test. You are never too young or too old to see what your hormones are doing! Books by Dr. John R. Lee and Virginia Hopkins, include *Men and Hormones, Hormones Made Simple, What Your Doctor May Not Tell You about Premenopause*, and *What Your Doctor May Not Tell You about Menopause*, and will give you a basis for understanding how hormones in your body work…or don't work. Another great source is a book by Sara Gottfried called Hormone Cure. And though women are more often thought of in connection with hormone imbalance, men are just as susceptible, with problems ranging from prostrate and bladder problems to migraines and sleep disturbances.

If you do need hormone replacement, go for the bio-identical hormones and not the synthetic or horse urine versions. The latter hormones can do more harm in the long run, as the body does not always recognize their chemical composition and may treat the non-natural hormones as invaders. There is evidence that blood testing is not as conclusive as the saliva test, and the books will explain both the aforementioned in complete detail. If you start taking hormone supplements, you may not need to take them forever; sometimes they are only needed for a season in your life. Also, I've found exercise has helped greatly in regulating my hormones. The more I understood and participated, the better I felt. I became an active participant and truly felt like a prism. I slowly got my shine back.

One note about anemia: My anemia was not picked up on the regular complete blood panel check. I continued to be severely fatigued and left out of breath from even the small tasks of carrying laundry up a flight of steps or walking from one side of the house to the other. One doctor didn't like these symptoms and sent me for a ferritin blood panel; this panel checks the *reserve* iron verses the everyday fluctuating iron. Even though I had a low-normal on the main panel, I was extremely low on the ferritin panel, which explained my continued fatigue and breathlessness. Insufficient iron levels may be caused from many things, including thyroid. Being hypothyroid can result in a lowered production of hydrochloric stomach acid, which in turn leads to the poor absorption of iron and nutrients from food or supplements. Also, being hypothyroid lowers your body temperature, which causes you to make fewer red blood cells, which in turn can cause anemia. If you take vitamin C along with an iron or vitamin supplement, the nutrients are better absorbed. I learned that dark berries of all kinds (blackberries, bilberries, blueberries) and spinach tend to bind and pull iron out of the body, even though they are loaded with iron. So if you are trying to get your iron levels up, you may wish to choose other iron fortified foods *for a little while.* I want to emphasize I am not a doctor, and I am sharing what many doctors advised me to do over the years. Speak with your own doctors and get their suggestions into your own personal issues. While you are at the doctor's, ask for a complete blood panel check if you are feeling too tired for life and your life is not severely stressed.

I have also learned that not only is a sublingual B-12 supplement (tablet, drops, or spray) good for repairing nerve damage, it is also good for helping build red blood cells, which helps anemic people. Some people even get a B-12 shot regularly. There is strong evidence the methylcobalamin B12's are a much better choice for healing.

Investigate your B-12 and iron supplements. The best iron supplement I've found has been an elemental iron made from an amino-acid chelate. If constipation seems to follow taking an iron supplement, take a magnesium citrate or extra vitamin C to soften your stools. The prescription (RX) iron supplements made me severely ill, and the ingredient succinic acid messed up my stomach and esophagus for months. When you investigate the ingredients and experience the side effects as I did, you can't help but ask why a flammable and corrosive product like succinic acid could be approved and used in a prescription supplement! So please, exercise common sense: just because a doctor says you need a supplement doesn't mean you will be able to safely take it. Don't override your body's wisdom when it tells you there's a problem. You may have to seek out other brands and other vitamin and mineral selections, or prescription choices.

Get plenty of sleep. You can accomplish more with a rested body. Listen to your body when it urges you to sleep. Don't listen to those friends who tell you can sleep when you are dead. If you don't get the needed sleep that helps your immune system, you just may be dead and sleeping before your time! Sleep is so beneficial in boosting your immune system, memory, metabolism, physical body, and other vital functions. Just as you need to eat, drink, breathe, and laugh, you need to sleep. Most of us don't realize just how much sleep we need to stay at our optimum ability to be "in" life. When you are an adult, the average sleep requirement is eight hours. The younger you are, the more hours you need. If you eat less at night, you will sleep better. Try to sleep without lights on, as light interferes with the "feel good hormones", melatonin and serotonin your brain makes in the darkness of night. If you can't achieve darkness in your room, try wearing an eye mask. Quieting the sleeping environment is also beneficial. Having music or television on all night will interfere with a good sleep cycle, even if you do fall asleep. Some televisions come with a sleep timer that will automatically shut the TV off in thirty minutes or an hour. Some CD players will automatically shut off, too. You can listen to stories or soothing music or watch your show to wind down, and the devices will automatically turn off. If you live in a noisy environment, a white noise machine drowns out noises nicely. Turn out the lights and eliminate excess noise, and maybe you can get a good night's sleep.

Find a good multivitamin and mineral supplement. View taking these as a little insurance policy for your health. Finding a good supplement can be exasperating because there are so many available with such a diversity of ingredients. If you cannot tolerate a supplement, don't feel pressured into taking it because your body may be telling you something. You may not need a supplement at this time in your life or the by-products in the supplement may be causing allergies. One man's necessary find may be another man's poison. Once, when I had a horrible cold, many people suggested Echinacea. For days I swallowed the supplement and/or drank the tea. Each time I did this, I ignored my gut instinct and felt even worse. I stopped taking the herb and immediately improved. Others swore by the benefits of the product, but my body just couldn't handle it. Vitamin C and zinc were a better choice for me. Just as I had to experiment, you may need to try different brands and different ingredients to find the right supplement for you.

A good way to test a vitamin's digestibility is to drop it into a glass of water for fifteen minutes. If it does not dissolve within that time, you may wish to find another supplement. You may find a supplement is only needed a few times a week, not daily, depending on your diet. I know some adults who take a children's multivitamin and nothing more. Take cues from your body and its health.

I would like to mention something from my own vitamin searches and the filler product magnesium stearate, which can also be listed as stearic acid, vegetable stearate, or brominated vegetable stearate. I have found this ingredient may irritate the stomach and intestinal lining, trigger allergic reactions, and reduce absorption of the supplement in question by seventy percent if too much of it is used in creating the supplement. When I discovered this, I threw out over half of my supplements and purchased others. I stopped getting the "normal" stomachache after taking my supplements. It is amazing how one minuscule ingredient will adversely affect the value of a good product! After finding a good supplement, if it still upsets your stomach, try taking it along with food and see if it helps solve the problem.

Also, if you have a corn sensitivity, ascorbyl (corn) palmitate (palm) can originate from either corn or palm. You may need to contact the company to verify this.

The B vitamin is a good stand-alone supplement. They can admittedly be a little smelly and hard to get past your nose, especially if you are sensitive to smells, so you may need to give them a sniff test! There is strong evidence that a complete B vitamin is very beneficial for stress and for repairing damaged cells. During one hectic time in my life I truly understood the value of a B vitamin. I'd had a crazy week, and this day was just another crazy continuation. As I was coming home from picking up one son to connect to another son's pick-up, I got a phone call letting me know my mother had locked herself out of her house. I got to her as soon as I could, and I even managed to visit with her a little afterward. We talked about the crazy week I was having! She handed me her vitamin B supplements. I hit the bottle of B vitamins that day and never looked back. As hectic as that day was for me, I was thankful my mother had locked herself out because I was given the opportunity to learn a good lesson in supplements. I can't believe I thought I was above life and stress! On the days when I am tired and my adrenals ache, I take two to three B supplements.

When you begin looking for supplements, read the labels, as all supplements will have different amounts of the vitamin, mineral, or herb being used. Also, don't feel that taking a "stress vitamin" allows you to make room for more stressors in your life. Supplements are only to help you smooth out the edges of crazy times and are not meant to allow you to pack more in. When you are tired, you need to rest, not drink more caffeine. Caffeine may get you to the time and place so you can rest, but then you need to rest. When you are stressed, you need to lessen the stress, not pop more vitamins. Taking a few extra supplements may help you get through the busy time, but once the busyness is over, you need to lighten the stress. Your body has its own profound wisdom and will lead you to what it needs. Listen to it.

Drink water! That is one of the best pieces of advice I can give. Depending on age, gender, and body structure, the human body is 50-77 percent. Our brains have the highest percent water content, but even our bones hold 10 percent. Water leaves us through sweat, bathroom visits, breath evaporation, tears, saliva, bleeding, sebum production, sickness (fever, vomiting, diarrhea), menstruation, reproductive fluids, and internal heat dissipation, so it is important to replace this loss daily. Have you ever forgotten to water a potted plant and later seen the evidence of your forgetfulness in the shriveled-up leaves and stems? Can you picture what your body looks like without its water? There are many differing suggestions as to the amount of liquids a person needs per day. One suggestion is, you should drink half your body weight in ounces, and so if you weighed one hundred and forty pounds, you would need approximately seventy ounces. If you know in your mind and heart, though, that your body needs more, give yourself some wholesome liquids. If you feel healthy without the suggested ounces, let that be okay too. You know better than anyone. If you are not sure, ask the following questions. Does your mouth feel dry or does your skin lack plumpness? Is your skin itchy and dry? Do your eyes not have that twinkling shine? Does it hurt when you breathe because your lungs do not have moisture? Are your lips dry and cracked? Is your nose dry, sore, stuffy, or bleeding? Does the skin peel on your hands and feet from dehydration? Positive answers to these questions could be indicators you need more H_2O.

Sometimes my stomach gets nauseas on just water, so I squeeze a little lemon or some other flavor into my glass. I will also put a pinch of sea salt in my water as this also helps lessen the nausea. The sea salt with natural minerals in it is *not the same* as table salt. Regular table salt can be dangerous to salt-restricted diets. Do not exceed more than one teaspoon of sea salt per day in your water.

It may help to set out a few extra filled glasses of water so you can visibly see where you are throughout the day. Find a beautiful pitcher or water jug and fill it with the amount of water you want to drink during the day. It is not good to drink all your allotment in one sitting to get it over with or because you forgot throughout the day. Too much water at once causes the blood to become too diluted and also places a lot of stress on the lungs and heart. Also, don't guzzle right before bed as you will be awakening throughout the night for frequent bathroom trips. Drink your water throughout the day and make it fun. If you forget, see if you can do better the next day. Drinking water or healthy fluids will maintain muscle mass, reduce sodium buildup, suppress appetite, reduce fatigue, aid bowel elimination, and help burn fat. I take a glass of water to bed with me and drink it as soon as I get up. I am hooked on that glass of water first thing in the morning; it replaces the water lost throughout the night and jump starts my metabolism. You will be pleasantly amazed how this simple glass of water first thing in the morning will help shed those pounds you have been trying to lose. If you get hot flashes in the night, water cools the body down quickly. After my shower, I get a cup of coffee, but throughout the day I drink my water. (Remember that drinking caffeine products will not necessarily replace the fluids because caffeine also dehydrates. If you drink caffeine products, you will need more water than people who don't.)

If you do sports, work in the heat, or are out in the heat, you need more liquid than the norm. Don't wait too long to replenish, as it is harder to recover from a severe loss than to just keep sipping. Drink clean water. Even if your publicly provided community water is low on chemicals, the water still contains chemicals your body doesn't need. Purify, filter, or alkalize your water. Drinking out of plastic may not be the best choice, either. We have all read or seen how plastic has a storehouse of chemicals in it that can disrupt your hormones. Definitely do not freeze, heat up, or reuse cheap water bottles. The chemicals in the bottles leach more over time and with temperature change. Even storing these types of bottles in a cold or hot car has the same effect. Purchase BPA-free plastic bottles which do not cause hormone disruptions. I laughed over a comment someone made from another country. She said, "America is one of the only countries who buy their water twice." Can you find ways to purify your tap water and safely store in little to-go bottles so you can safely use your own clean water? Whatever way you get your water, enjoy your next glass!

    Can you start eating better? This can be very difficult, especially if you have had years of unhealthy eating habits. Habits can be so hard to change because they feel so comfortable. You don't need to get rid of all your comfort foods; you only need to incorporate healthy foods, too. Have patience with your taste buds as they are learning to incorporate new tastes. Picture a new baby as it tries and spits out new foods. The baby makes many comical faces as it learns to appreciate the taste and value of food. Eventually, your taste buds will stop revolting against your efforts to introduce them to new and healthy tastes. As you scout for good eating choices, shop as much as you can around the parameter of the grocery store, where healthier foods are more often located. Processed foods usually do not need refrigeration because of the preservatives in them, so they are usually towards the center of the store without refrigeration. When shopping for canned goods, continue to read labels to find out how they are preserved. Processed foods and preservatives wreak havoc on a body, dragging you down. The preservatives in processed foods extend shelf-life, but they do not extend the self-life of you.

    Eat as much uncooked and uncorrupted food as you can. Watch out for foods and drinks loaded with corn sugars and regular sugars. Try to stay away from genetically modified foods (GMOs), like soy, corn, and peanut products, which are so altered our bodies don't always recognize them. Coffee and teas can be grown with many chemicals and pesticides. Know the sources of your beverages and buy accordingly. Try to incorporate fresh and organic foods. If you eat processed or cooked meats, try to incorporate raw vegetables and fruits, too. Uncooked vegetables and fruits have enzymes that aid in the digestion process. Try to see how you can eat as much unprocessed and raw food as you can. Know that your dietary needs can also change from one stage of your life to the next, so stay alert to any intestinal or digestion issues that arise. Assess your food choices periodically. As a person ages, stomach acid can decrease. That may be a good time to incorporate a digestive enzyme along with those raw vegetables and fruits in your meals.

You can tell if fresh fruits and vegetables are commercially grown, genetically modified, or organically grown by their labels. If the item doesn't have a sticker, look at the store sign for the 4 or 5 digit number that applies.

If the number is:
- 4 digits, the food is conventionally grown
- 5 digits starting with an 8, the food is genetically modified
- 5 digits starting with a 9, the food is organically grown

Here are a few other suggestions. Try to remove harmful beauty and household products from your life. Look into your shampoos, makeup, shaving creams, deodorants, perfumes, nail polishes and removers, and household cleaners. Some of the chemicals in them can cause respiratory distress, contact dermatitis, allergies, hormone disruption, and cancer. Fluorescent lights can disrupt your energy field in detrimental ways, so if you have a choice in your lighting design, you may want to research what alternatives work best for you. Spectra Mineral Lights are an excellent lighting option as they help with seasonal depression that can occur because of lack of sunlight.

Don't give up everything because we are meant to enjoy life, but start to notice what you eat, wear, and surround yourself with, as the chemicals used in manufacturing all these things can cause allergic reactions that leave you feeling sick. Some people are just more sensitive to chemicals than are others. Also, don't believe "organic" always means "the best." You can find organic foods and products that just are not kosher or are still genetically modified. Read the labels carefully!

I wear certain jewelry or gems to help me. At the time of this writing, I am wearing a pink moonstone to help with some female issues. Men and women wear magnetic, copper, or ion bracelets and necklaces to help with certain issues, too. One book I like, *Healing Crystals and Gemstones* by Dr. Flora Peschek-Bohmer and Gisela Schreiber, has color pictures for stone identification and quick references telling you how the stone helps in healing. A small local shop provides me with some great gemstone jewelry; you may have a similar shop near you.

Mental imagery or picturing yourself in a serene place is a great way to de-stress. You might picture a beach, a cabin, a snow-covered oasis, a favorite fishing hole, or serenely motoring down a road. You can also picture your body being cleansed. Some people picture their cancer being washed out of them by cool water starting from the head and running to their feet. Some picture their cells bright and pink, energetic and healthy. You can even visualize the chakra colors up and down your body. Do these visualizations with only the allowing intention of enjoying your life and body. This means, don't imagine what is lacking. Only imagine what is happening in that visualization, or what you are wishing to happen at that moment for your physical and spiritual self.

I have a set of Oracle cards, which come in a deck and usually have anywhere from twenty to fifty cards. My set, *Archangel Michael Oracle Cards*, is one of many sets by Doreen Virtue. This is the set I referred to in the Angel chapter. These cards may sit a year before I need to use them, but when I am unable to calm my thoughts or need guidance on a perplexing matter, I select a card for help and direction, and the card is like a little pep talk. There are many different kinds of Oracle cards; pick a deck you can enjoy, either for the art work or the sayings.

Check out a marvelous book, *Handwriting Can Change Your Life*, by Vimala Rodgers. She also has a workbook and CD available. This awesome handwriting program can help you reprogram your subconscious, just by making purposeful shifts in your handwriting. After years of studying and researching handwriting, Rodgers developed a writing system to bring out hidden talents, abilities, and peace. You can find and release self-limiting patterns, then change them to self-affirming patterns. The technique helps clear blockages, heal old wounds, and express your creativity. If you are trying to find your creative outlet, this book may well help you. All it takes is pen, paper, and practice. Rodgers helps people confirm they are no longer bystanders in their own lives. I had an idea I wanted to write, but I never fully felt it until I started her writing exercises. I felt motivated and everything shifted for me in a truly meaningful way. Within a month of practicing Rodgers' writing suggestions, I started writing this book. My son never complains now about doing his writing homework using Rodgers' methods, but he did complain about all the other writing workbooks we used, so out of the mouth of babes comes the truth! He and I have found a winner.

As I was writing this book, I encouraged my sister to soak in a tub of Epsom salts, since I felt she would benefit from Epsom salts' amazing properties. Afterward, she asked that I include baths in my book as most don't think of a bath as having benefits. So, I will elaborate. Epsom salts is named after a spring in Epsom, England, and is not a salt but a rich hydrated magnesium sulfate. It has amazing health benefits in that it can ease stress and relax the body. This mineral can be poorly absorbed by the stomach, and soaking in the tub may be the answer to acquiring enough, since the magnesium sulfate can be absorbed directly through the skin. This mineral plays an important role in the functioning of brain tissue, joint proteins, and the proteins that line the walls of the digestive tract. It stimulates the pancreas to generate digestive enzymes, and it helps detoxify your body of environmental or medicinal toxins. If you are diabetic, or have hypertension or a heart condition, rinse off after the bath. Add two cups of Epsom salts and soak for ten minutes about three times a week to notice benefits.

There are other types of baths you may also wish to try. I was told about one grandmother who would soak in sea salt baths when she couldn't swim in the ocean. Sea salt baths, like ocean water, helped alleviate her arthritis symptoms. There are many other bath choices; oatmeal, apple cider vinegar, baking soda, ground mustard, other herbs, and clay baths are all options. Different baths help different conditions and can be used to detoxify, calm allergic reactions like poison ivy or chicken pox, cure eczema and some funguses, ease sunburns, help sore muscles, increase circulation, and ease arthritis. Do some research, and enjoy a bath every once in a while.

They say health is all a state of mind, and this is so true. You can eat the healthiest foods in the world and wear the purest of clothing but still be sick. If you are eating an organic apple with discontent, you are no healthier—and maybe worse off—than the person eating a Snickers bar with much happiness. You see, everything is all relative. We are what we eat, but we are also what we believe, think, and feel.

Please don't think that I am super-human and have it all together all the time. I have learned them over many years, but I don't always remember to use them! We are all going to apply what we remember or feel compelled to use. I have only attempted to give you tools for your box or an outfit to try on, so to speak. What tool you pull out, or what outfit you wear on any given day, is what you evidently need. If you chose to call in a subcontractor or a seamstress, that is your choice, too. Hopefully, whatever you use will get you moving in a positive direction. For mental and physical health, once again, you need to find what will work for you, what has a nice fit and flow and is of ease. If new ways of thinking and being are attempted with anxiety or resentment, no amount of "good" you are doing will bring you health. Find your own ease, and pace yourself into it.

*"There are no unnatural or
supernatural phenomena,
only very large gaps in
our knowledge of what is natural."*
—Edgar Mitchell

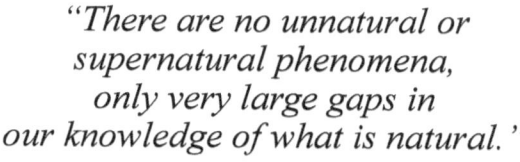

Astrology

Astrology involves the solar system and how it pertains to our life. Planets were created prior to man in preparation for man himself. Astrology is an energy delivery system, and planets deliver certain energies to be picked up at designated times in our lives, like a time-released vitamin pill. The pill gives you only a portion of the mineral, slowly, instead of all at once. At certain points in our lives, different planets give us their energy or support.

Astrology understands how these planets' energies are imprinted on us and what the next flow of planetary energy will give us. It does not use the planets to predict the future. Predictions and astrology are two completely different activities. Predictions use your body's energy to try to read your future. Even though some predictions can be very accurate, they are guesses just the same. If a person changes her energy into light or darkness, then the predictions may not reflect the recent energy shift. Astrology on the other hand, uses the solar system's stable and unconditional energy that is flowing to you to show in what ways planets may be influencing you.

Planets are familiar to us; we learned about them in science class, and some of them we can see just by looking up into the sky. Astrology is based on where all the planets were at the exact time, date, and location of your birth. It is very personal, like your fingerprint. Where the Sun, Moon, Venus, Mars, Jupiter, Mercury, Neptune, Pluto, Saturn, Chiron, and Uranus were at the time of my birth will be different from where they were at the time of your birth. I thought for so long that if you raise your children the same way then, surely, they would all be the same. My children were not all the same, even though I treated and raised them in the same manner. I didn't know why until I took a quick introductory class on astrology. I then understood why all my children are beautifully different, why my husband is who he is, and why I am the way I am.

Don't be afraid of the planets for they are here to help in your life's journey. Documented astrology has been used for well over three thousand years. Some very fanatic and religious people frown on astrology, but even King David and King Solomon in the Bible used a form of astrology for support. Astrology does not tell you what to do in your life, as we are free willed humans, but it does give you some concrete features your life takes on. Astrology is like a road map. You are the vehicle, unique in your own make, model, and year. Your free will lets you choose which route to take and how you wish to proceed.

Planets are amazing, and they are used more than we realize. Some people plant gardens by the moon, others try new endeavors on new moons, and babies are born when the moon changes into a full moon or new moon. Some even cut their lawns or hair at certain times to retard or enhance hair and lawn growth. Some fish and hunt at certain times based on this same concept. *The Farmer's Almanac*, which is a wonderfully informative and fun book, forecasts the weather for sixteen months using a long-standing formula of many factors like moon phases, sunspots, and so on. Just another way the planets have, once again, been very useful to and for us.

Astrology is like weather forecasting. You take in many different factors to make an astrological analysis. First, you have your sun sign (Aries, Taurus, Gemini, Cancer, Leo, Virgo, Libra, Scorpio, Sagittarius, Capricorn, Aquarius, & Pisces), and then you figure if the planets have strong or weak influences. Astrologers understand how a planet's location influences other planets, as well as how long a planet stays in each house (or period of your development). There is a lot to factor into an astrological analysis, and many little things that need to be understood. For example, your sun sign may be Taurus, but you may have more characteristics of another sign in your houses that make you feel more like a Gemini. As you see, astrology is so personal and intricate that something like the newspaper's daily horoscope could not possibly represent a clear picture of who you really are. A knowledgeable astrologer, one who looks into all the intricacies of each individual chart, can help you understand who you really are and help you uncover your abilities and hidden talents. An astrologer is like a detective who looks at all kind of details, from bold, noticeable details to tiny, infinitesimal details. Astrology entails diligence and study; it is not merely reading a book and forecasting. Because astrology is a complicated and demanding practice, I recommend getting reviews from others before you decide if a certain astrologer is for you.

Also, remember that even if you were born the same day, second, and location as another person, you are not exactly alike. I understand that because I am a twin. Our charts are almost identical. We are very much alike, yet very different. Our genetic, past life experiences, and personalities also play a role in who we are and who we are becoming. Astrology is the mere outline of your portrait. The other things, just mentioned, truly give us our vibrant color that fills in astrology's definitive outline. My twin and my outlines are almost exact, but our color inside is different. I also liken astrology to a black and white photograph, while your genetics and everything you have lived is the color version. Please remember this and don't be tempted to place everyone you know into cookie cutter versions of their astrological signs.

Here's a very quick run through of the zodiacs (sun signs):

Aries - *"I am"* - Most self-oriented. Energies concentrated on self-development, leadership qualities and ideas. *Needs*: to test themselves. March 21-April 19

Taurus - *"I have"* - Value what they have, sensuous, stubborn and loyal. Can be very possessive of stuff. *Needs*: physical security. April 20-May 20

Gemini - *"I think"* - Mental explorers. Communicators. Gets bored easily and likes change. *Needs*: freedom and exploration. May 21-June 21

Cancer - *"I feel"* - Mothering. Takes care of and is the nurturing sign. Very deep feeling. *Needs*: emotional security. June 22-July 22

Open Your Heart to the True You

Leo - *"I will"* - Self-expression. Inner power & strength. Leo the Lion. Fixed ideas. *Needs*: respect and appreciation. July 23-August 22

Virgo - *"I analyze"* - Purists! Looks at things microscopically. Collects, digests, and correlates facts. Will get it done; driven. *Needs*: to be known as expert in field. August 23-Sept. 22

Libra - *"I balance"* - Very social, peacemakers, strong sense of fair play. Into partnerships and beauty of all things. Sees all sides. *Needs*: social acceptance. Sept. 23- Oct. 22

Scorpio - *"I desire"* - Strong creative desires. Can be withdrawn, intense, and possessive. Sees things hidden underneath. *Needs*: meaningful connections and devotion. Oct. 23-Nov. 21

Sagittarius - *"I see"* - About philosophy and big ideas. Talkative and forward thinking. *Needs*: fun and freedom to grow. Nov. 22-Dec. 21

Capricorn - *"I Use"* - Fathering. Builds from ground up with a good foundation. Takes duty and responsibility seriously. *Needs*: to belong to the world. Dec. 22-Jan. 19

Aquarius - *"I Know"* - Friendships and group activities. Unconventional and strong willed. Humanitarian. *Needs*: freedom to be self. Jan. 20-Feb. 18

Pisces - *"I Believe"* - Sensitive and devoted. Open, creative, and psychic. Deeply emotional, introspective & compassionate. *Needs*: to be alone for contemplation. Feb. 19-Mar. 20

The Exquisite Zodiac, by Rick DiClemente with Liza Jane Brown, is a fun and easy book to read, and it explains sun signs very well. They also have a website at starself.com. Another great astrologer I have grown to love is Camille Albrecht, and her website is camillealbrecht.com. They are knowledgeable astrologers, and I recommend them to anyone. There are, of course, many, many other good astrologers, and I hope you will be just as blessed as I was in finding one.

Have fun as you learn about yourself and/or your loved ones. Planets are useful and very active in each and every one of our lives, whether we realize and acknowledge it or not. They are yet another silent support system given to us.

*"Yesterday, I was clever so I wanted to
change the world.
Today, I am wise so I am changing myself."*
—Zahid Iqbal Khan (Rumi)

Closing

Passage to health requires personal change. View change as the one constant in your life. Expect it. Anticipate it. Welcome it. In seasons of change, we find new and better ways as well as the necessary tools to maintain our health and soul. Once, when I was fretting over time, my mother-in-law told me, "Rome wasn't built in a day." Most of us have seen pictures of how beautiful Rome was and still is, but it took years to become what it is now. Let your beautiful life unfold and be built, not in one day, but throughout your lifetime. Old habits don't need to be eliminated all at once; you can slowly replace them with habits more in tune to who you are becoming.

The healing you need will come in future days and months. Life will continually become clearer to you as you participate in change. Try not to get discouraged because sometimes, no matter how much light you carry in your soul, there will still be times of feeling you are in the darkness of confusion. The changes you go through may also seem awkward. Remember when you moved into a new residence how many times, out of habit, you started to travel the old established road back to the old address? The old route and residence were a comfortable habit. Your new paths and insights will also feel less awkward in time. Eventually, they will be the comfortable, well-worn road back home. Remember too, that you are only human, not super-human like most of us would like to be, so have patience. Like a radio tuner, you will need to adjust your mental knob when you pick up static, old thought patterns, or negativity. Keep patient while tuning to your connection because you can bring yourself into clarity.

Growing can be hard, and it can seem like just so much frustration. It's like a baby's growth experience. The infant looks so forward to growing (sitting, crawling, walking, and running), that it continues to do these things, even with the sore muscles, bumps, and bruises. Those "ouch" moments are so beneficial to the child's forward advancement! I still get sore mental muscles, bumps, and bruises like that baby, but the discomfort is needed for my own forward growth. Sometimes, you will even have fun experiencing growth, and you will be able to smile through the frustration. Picture the baby who takes a few steps only to thump down hard on his bottom. The child may sit there smiling with accomplishment and fun, even with a sore bottom. Either way, in fun or frustration, there is true liberation from these new and unexplored paths because there really is only one way to go… forward!

In moving forward, you will begin to have little pieces of consciousness of many things you have longed to understand. These little pieces will come only when needed and at the right time. Try not to over think them as this can overwhelm you. Casually allow the pieces to flow, like a breath that comes in and goes back out. The breath supports you, but it doesn't stay around long. Sometimes, it may be hard to see what picture all those little consciousness pieces are ultimately making because you are inside the frame, or the confines, of your expectations. Get out of the confines, and casually view your life. Then, you can reflect and clearly arrange the many pieces. Eventually, more and more pieces will appear, and the picture will become clearer.

Life is not always perfect, so finding your happiness, truths, and advancements need not depend on perfection. You are already excellent just as you are. You are only now fine-tuning. So keep moving forward to those things you want. The truths you seek will be what resonate within your soul. Your truth will not be the same as another person's truth. There is no one single truth, as there is no one single personality. You are the one to create your own truths. If you hold a truth, or do something because you believe it is good, it will benefit you. If you do something in fear, or if you do something you feel is bad for you, or if you do something only because someone else wants you to do it, it will have a negative effect on you. You are here to learn, live, have fun, and uncover your truths. Find *your* truth of what *you* need and what feels good.

You are no longer a passive victim of yourself or others. No more being a victim; be victorious. You have the right and the skills to rise above and change everything in your day to day situations and relationships. As long as you blame others or believe that they control you, you will remain stuck. As long as you feel you can't, you won't. You get to decide. Also, if something is happening now that is not good, you can find a way to change, even if only by thought. If things are going well for you, focus on this and how this well- being will continue. You can make your today's story even better, even if only in thought, so don't keep repeating your history unless it is a story you want to keep. Live the life you envision. William Ernest Henley, in his beautiful poem, "Invictus," wrote, "It matters not how straight the gate. How charged with punishment the scroll. I am the master of my fate. I am the captain of my soul." You can build on being victorious because you are your own captain.

You have more *understanding* and *tools* to support you today than you did yesterday. You are wiser today. You are improving with each tiny baby step. Go slowly, like a baby taking its first steps. Please, don't try all these suggestions at once! It could prove very overwhelming and cause you to give up, like doing algebra before you learned basic math concepts, or trying to run a mile race before you even learned to jog around the block. It could cramp you up terribly, and create havoc on your internal system.

As you go forward, look back at your earliest stages of growth and be amazed as you compare your beginning to where you have progressed. Just don't assess too frequently, as that can be discouraging if you are not where you think you should be. When you reflect over a long span of time, there is more progress for you to see and be encouraged by. So keep moving, and don't spend too much time looking back. In fact, some people don't even look back at all. They just know where they are going with the feeling of freedom, and any looking back only pulls them back.

We all know what we need to do for our advancement or enlightenment, but it is indeed one thing to know, and quite another thing to put that knowledge into daily practice. This is like the phrases we have heard so many times: *What you do speaks louder than what you say. Practice what you preach.*

We know it, but we don't do it. The bottom line is, the power to choose and exercise your truths is within your own mind and power, but you have to do it. Lip service will get you nowhere.

Never expect to be finished learning. There is a Zen Proverb, "What do you do before enlightenment? I chop wood and carry water. What do you do after enlightenment? I chop wood and carry water." Keep moving forward. Here is to each of us and our accomplishments, big and small! With love and my best to you, my friends!

May Your Heart Be Light,
—Renee

Open Your Heart to the True You

-Sometimes
it's the most beautiful flowers
in the garden that can take the
longest to grow.-

-Anonymous-

An excerpt from *Open Your Mind to the True You*
by Renee Salvatori…

"We can out-distance that which is running after you, but not that what is running inside you."
—Rwandan Proverb

Fear

The acronym for FEAR is: Feeling Excited And Ready. That is when it is a healthy fear. When we can feel excited and ready. Are you ready to face your fear? Are you excited to look at it in a way you hadn't in a while? There is a freedom when we are proactive in any situation verses just letting things or thoughts randomly play out in our psyche.

There is a saying that courage doesn't always roar but that it can be a silent movement into something that scares you. Move forward gently and serenely looking into your fears. Let them look back at you so that you see them as a clear picture. In the clarity, you may be able to abolish or minimize your fear and worries. You can stay focused in yesterday, even if it is because of fear. You can stay paralyzed in the now because of fear. You can be focused on the what-ifs of tomorrow because of fear. What good is all this focus on fear? It is good to work through it so you have more time for healthier and positive things.

Fear is a common barrier that keeps us from living our lives fully. If you live in fear, you are not free to take risks to pursue your dreams and desires. If your fear is on failure, rejection, or criticism, that is where your energy lies, when your energy should be in making your dreams happen. Are you playing safe behind your fears instead of making your goals happen?

Insecurities and fears (perceived or real) and fear of change, can give us constant pain in the pit of our stomach. It has killed more dreams and success than any other ailment. Some people sabotage their success because of it. People have lost their voice over fear, couldn't move because of fear, and even gave up on living because of fears. It can be the worst enemy of all human species. It is not something we ignore and act like it is not here. It is spoken about in the Bible, Koran, and Torah. It seems the older we get, the more we allow fear to fuel us. It becomes so common, we tend to ignore the gut and physical ills caused by it. We build up an immunity to its symptoms.

Fear is definitely real and can be viewed differently from person to person. Just as how one person can cry at a movie while another doesn't, fear is another emotion playing out uniquely in each life. It is, however, an emotion that doesn't always make one feel good and could even cripple you from fully living your life.

But we don't need to abolish our fears in order to be unchained by them; we just need to feel protected in analyzing them. Either embrace the desire to see where the fears came from and why, or resolve to be at peace with each fear.

An example: my son is terrified by spiders. He has thought about it and really doesn't know where the fear came from. Yet, he is okay with the fact he is afraid of arachnids and thus chooses not to intentionally be in areas with them. That is the only peace he needs for his fear. When he sees a spider, he'll move away from it, but he does not allow the spider to control him.

Personally, I am fearful of mice. I know because I have had live run-ins with them where I have actually touched them. I can view them at pet stores peacefully, but I get very nervous if I know a mouse is running uncontained in my house. That is the only piece of analyzing my mouse fear I need to do. To recognize the fear and to know how I will react when confronted makes me more confident. Oh, I could go to therapy and/or take a hypnotizing session into allowing them to crawl in my hand without fear, but for me, this piece of knowledge is the only peace I need. Sometimes that *is* all you need with simple fears.

Instead of resisting the fear, one needs to acknowledge it. To say "stop the fear" is like saying, "don't be afraid of the spider," if you are truly terrified of spiders. If you are afraid of heights, convincing yourself that you shouldn't be is also a moot point. It is something that needs your attention as you are feeling it, as you are in that *aware* state of it. Only in awareness can it be dealt with consciously.

Zig Zigler once said, "Courage is not the absence of fear, but it's the mastery of it." That statement in itself implies it is something not to be ignored but worked with, as a fear is not something that will just go away.

I am afraid of heights because I may fall to my death. I am afraid of changing jobs because I may not make enough money. I am afraid of marriage because it may end in divorce. I am afraid to sign up for a class because I may not pass the test in the end. If you can label your fear and understand it, you are well on your way to changing how you handle your fears.

Sometimes fear builds momentum to the point it paralyzes us. It may be simple little fears that before you know it, pull you in heavily like quicksand, leaving you struggling to get out. Fears' momentum can even imprison us in our own homes.

But remember, you can always change the speed of momentum in the early stages: it is much harder to stop once it gets going.

Think of running down a hill. At the top of the hill, you will start out slower, then pick up speed as your feet quickly whisk you down-hill at what feels like warp speed. Sometimes even taking your feet from underneath you and rolling down the hill instead of running. The momentum will carry you without you even trying or exerting much effort.

Now, think of ways in your life where momentum can take over. By staying alert to momentum in situations, we can better gauge how we are doing. Now, momentum can be a friend to us if things are going well. By all means, allow the momentum to roll. If things are going badly, then quickly change its speed.

Think of the Winnie the Pooh literature. Little Piglet is a very little creature with fear bigger than itself. He constantly dealt with his fears to overcome them, but once he did, what a glorious celebration for such a little being. His bravery became much bigger than himself. Overcoming or dealing with fear is a triumphant event.

Here is another example of fear. When my one son started kindergarten within his first three days of school he became very sick. He got mononucleosis, or mono as most people call it. I knew it was mere coincidence and timing that made him sick, but in his mind, he believed it was school that did it. Thus began his fear of school. I did not realize how he had encapsulated many elements to his mono episode. Even the very food he ate the day he got sick became an item of fear along with the very shirt he wore. He was young and unable to redirect his initial fear. I did not foresee how his original fear compounded. If I could have a do-over, I would be smarter with my young son. I would have helped him orchestrate his fear before it rolled with its' momentum. Now that he is older, he understands better how his fears controlled him and is learning to overcome them.

If you are intellectually able to look at a fear, you can, in the first thirty seconds, decide how you will proceed with it. Are you going to let it build into something even more frightful? Or, will you try to defeat it? Once we allow it to build and encapsulate us, we allow it to trap us, and we begin to give too much energy and time to it. The fear becomes *bigger* and *badder* in our mind. That is why the first thirty seconds or the *firsts* of any fear should be zeroed in on.

Fear is a negative force a person can consciously or unconsciously use to either evolve or become stagnant. Fear has a raw power that can either paralyze or save lives. Taming or directing it is challenging. A fear of walking to your vehicle at night in a crime-active neighborhood will propel you to have your keys at the ready, while quickly getting yourself to your car or not parking in an alley. The fear of taking a new job, getting married, having your first child, etcetera, is a different type of fear—one where you are overcoming ignorance which the fear stems from, and therefore overcoming the fear of the change your new lifestyle will bring. The analyzing of it may not be as easy as having your car keys at the ready, but it still needs to be understood.

Fear can be a controlled force, *even while you are living your own reality at that very moment.* Like my daughter who is very fearful of needles. She manages to control her fear by deep breathing or holding a hand while having a procedure done. Your fears will expand or shrink with how you think and feel and grow throughout your entire life. Like my young son's fear of school will shrink the day he graduates, but may arise again the day he takes his own child to kindergarten. Fear will only have the power you give it. Don't feed your fear. You just need to stop the momentum and rise above its drama.

Think. Are you embellishing it? Are you able to become clear to its history? Can you replace any negative movies you are playing in your mind? If all you see are negative images of a change you are about to embark on or a particular situation repeatedly happening, replace it with positive ones; all the wonderful possibilities of the grand things that *could* happen instead of the negatives of a situation. Negativity only makes things worse.

Dealing with fear can be constant, and again it is not advised to avoid fear but to inspect it and see if it is your own insecurities that are nurturing it or allowing it to grow. Many times by diminishing our own internal images of it in our mind, we can lessen the oxygen we feed its flame and decrease it from a bon fire to a little smolder and maybe put it out altogether. When you are able to look into its core, you may quickly be able to extinguish the reasons why for some if its creation.

Fear can also destroy a romance before it has time to blossom. Shyness, or the fear of confrontation, can put a halt to becoming intimate with someone else. It can tangle your ideas even before they can emerge, and fear can end an adventure even before you can begin it. Sometimes concerns are reasonable, but other times they are simply echoes of our own unchecked fears. They can hinder you and your family from experiencing life.

Who can forget the classic line from the Old Testament that was delivered by Job, "That which I feared most has come upon me." (Job 2.) Did Job allow his mind to continually play out his fears? We will never know, but perhaps we can take to heart his wisdom of that sentence.

Franklin D. Roosevelt once said, "We have nothing to fear but fear itself." Fear can kill people's dreams and even people themselves. But like Roosevelt said, we have nothing to fear...

There was a story of a tribe who held a ceremony somewhat like how spin the bottle is played. During the ritual, whomever the bottle landed on was foreshadowed the victim of a disease or fallen future. The fear was so great that many would immediately die from a heart attack if the bottle landed on them. That is a perfect example of how fear can build up to monumental proportions in just seconds.

There is a famous saying that goes, "Feel the fear and do it anyway." However, that is only good in some situations. I had to approach a manager of a store once and I was extremely scared. I told myself, "Feel the fear and do it anyways." It was my mantra that I used to walk my jelly legs into the store. As I approached the manager and spoke my complaint, the fear of speaking to this authority figure went away.

A mantra may be good in situations where we need to push ourselves forward. We might tell our child who is afraid to speak to their teacher about a grade this mantra. We may need to tell ourselves that, as we approach our boss for a raise. You may tell yourself this little mantra as you psych yourself up to take the stage for a theatre play. But, walking down a dark alley or marrying someone you have second doubts about, is not where this saying fits in. Climbing a mountain, if you are afraid of heights, may also not be the opportunity to use that line. Testing and working with your fear will never compromise you. It will act as an improvement and not a detriment. Pay attention to what the fear tells you. Listen closely. Does it say, you need to move on and nail this, you are not quite ready, or is the fear an internal intuition that is guiding you to safety?

Let's take for instance the fear of a new job. How do you know the fear is an internal nagging that it is a wrong choice, verses fear of just the newness of the change? Is it just the normal worry fear—will my co-workers like me—or *true* intuition of it not being a good fit or timing of it? Start by thinking about that new job. When you think of *not* taking the job, does the fear ease up? If it diminishes and you feel better by seeing yourself not there, then avoid it and do not start the job. When you contemplate this new job and the fear stays the same or gets worse, it could be an indication of just mere nervousness of change. This formula works for most anything in determining good fear or general nervous fear.

Fear plays a huge part in whom we are and who we are becoming, and where we are going in life. We all have fear and we all handle fear differently. Fear can lurk in every corner of our world, town, and home. Some use fear for their advantage, while others hide from the smallest amount of fear. We can even become so comfortable with the way things are that we fear change. I am still trying to convince myself to get a Facebook page and learn how to use online marketing tools. I drag my feet because I fear change. Except, here is the truth, the only thing changing is everything around me, not myself. Everyone is evolving but me. So I constantly have to work on my fear of change. Maybe by the time you read this, I will have a Facebook page. I, too, am always a work in progress.

Change of anything can cause fear. Change can be looked at as an adventure rather than something that is wrong. New territories and new actions can be scary, but it can also challenge you to new ideas and revitalizing newness. Change keeps you young, while being rigid creates internal friction and blocks creativity. In its newness, be open and positive to see where things can go.

Insecurities can also breed fear. That is a fear that is like a computer virus, and it will slowly get into all your internal workings and destroy so much of your life if you do not stop it with your own fire protection wall.

Most of your fears are not even reality-based or deserving of thoughts. They are imagined and projected onto us by fantasized thoughts. They may ask you to move out of your comfort zone, like the fear of taking a class, making a commitment, etc. I almost allowed fear to stop me from taking an on-line class once. The fear that I wasn't smart enough to finish it or even pass it almost overcame me. It took me two months of self-talk and analyzing before I finally signed up. My son was scared to go to the Homecoming Dance with a date because he worried the girl would not like spending time with him the next day. So many little fears can hold us back in the same-old, same-old comfort zone without our even realizing it.

Sometimes to avoid change or newness we procrastinate and keep postponing. We explain all the reasons it won't work. We surround ourselves with others who will confirm to us just why it won't work and we become convinced it won't work.

Surrounding yourself with unsupportive people is not the answer. Once you identify that fear and avoidance is holding you back, you can then do the opposite action that will help you over-ride those old thought patterns and overcome your fears. Find reasons why something *can work*, look for people who will agree with you that it will work, and socialize with those who support you. You can live boldly and bring your heartfelt goals into fruition. You may only need to play it out differently than what naturally feels normal.

Many fears can also be fears handed down from a caregiver, parent, relative, or other important person in our lives. Stay alert to those, too, as they are just as real. Once you begin to acknowledge and analyze those fears, you will understand a self-defeating or sabotaging behavior and put it into your own context and if you should rightfully hold onto it. An example of a widely spread, handed-down fear is the fear of God. Many hold close to the idea of a vengeful, conditional, unforgiving God. We fear His punishment, wrath, anger, vindication and violence. Why has time allowed this belief to brew into such deep fear? We can allow ourselves the time to examine God from our own true heartfelt place, instead of what others have fed us or transposed in written scriptures. God is common-sense and forgiving just as our thoughts should be of Him. We need to stop killing in God's name and fearing such a wonderful Light. But it is again, up to each of us to analyze this internal fear passed on to see where it fits in our lives.

Think of the boat that is safely anchored at the harbor. It is built to navigate the ocean, winds and rains, yet it stays there to ensure its safety because of fear. But that is not what boats are built to do. We are like boats, built to navigate life and take in all its' opportunities. Occasionally we dock in the harbor to build our courage and restock, but we sail back out of its confines.

What are some examples of your fears? Replace any negative movies you are playing in your mind with positive images. Find all the possibilities of the grand things that *could* happen. Be open. Be imaginative. Be you. Do not let fear rule who you are or keep you anchored at the dock. Are you ready to acknowledge your fear? Are you excited and ready to see it in a new way: F.E.A.R. (feeling excited and ready)?

If you enjoyed Renee Salvatori's story, check out this Spring 2017 Release from Written Dreams Publishing!

News from Lake Boobbegone
A Breast Cancer Memoir from the Heart

Carolyn Redman

"As a cancer survivor myself, I found myself completely immersed in this very poignant memoir from beginning to end. Ms. Redman shared her story so honestly and with such vulnerability; by the end I felt transported into her personal "Oz". I would recommend this book to anyone looking to gain insight into the cancer 'trip'."
—Maria Voermans, Wellness Coordinator

**Question: Does the world really need another breast cancer memoir?
Answer: Probably not.**
But writing is the only way Carolyn Redman knew how to process a heartbreaking breast cancer diagnosis and the year-long treatments that ensued. These honest, heartfelt, and sometimes humorous e-mails and essays, written solely to keep family and friends informed of her medical condition morphed into the definitive exercise in self-compassion and healing. In the end, no one was more surprised or more grateful than she was to find purpose and meaning masquerading as cancer.

Glossary

Acupressure-Applying pressure or light touch to areas of the body to increase the flow of energy and blood supply. Reflexology is a form of acupressure.

Acupuncture-The insertion of tiny needles to encourage the flow of energy along the body's meridian lines. It can be used with heat or electrical stimulus.

Astral-Of or like the stars. Can also refers to celestial.

Astrology-The science of the planets. Astrology is the relationship between the heavenly bodies and us. It uses the position of the planets and stars in the sky to help us understand the past, present, and future within the universe. Planetary influences affect the very moment you took your first breath.

Aum-Not necessarily a word but a vibration; does not belong to any language. Like the word OM, it can be used as a mantra for meditation, calming, and quiet.

Aura-An invisible vapor that surrounds a person, animal, or living object. There are many colors and layers, and the layers expand outward. The aura can be referred to as the etheric body, energetic double, or sphere of energy. It can serve as a filter for you or as an antenna.

Clairaudience-Clear hearing—When you hear music, name, or a conversation that seems made just for you. You might hear a song on the radio that holds a meaning, a high pitched ringing in ears, or a voice in your head or outside your ears. People with clairaudience are very sensitive to noise and sound.

Clair cognizance-Clear knowing—When you just know. You say or write with wisdom exceeding your years or knowledge. You might have brilliant ideas, or you know how to fix an item without reading instructions.

Clairsentience-Is a clear feeling, gut feeling, tingling sensation, goose bumps, or a hunch. You tend to be extra sensitive to energy, others' feelings, and/or chemicals. Be careful who you spend time with, as you are affected by others' presences more than the average person.

Clairvoyance-Clear seeing—You can see sparkling or flashing light or mind movies that provide clear wisdom while awake or asleep. You may be sensitive to light or color in the physical world.

Counselor-Advisor; involves two people working together to solve an issue. There are many forms of advice giving such as financial planning, spiritual guidance, religious help, and so on. Just about anyone can be a counselor.

Crystals-Are a natural and earth element that has energy. Crystals can be used to heal. Watches can run on quartz.

Cult-To some the word cult conjures up images of strangely dressed people with shaved heads and tambourines chanting, or a small group of extremists with charismatic leaders, like those who have had mass suicides. Yet to some, even Jesus and his disciples can be described as a cult among the Jews in their day. Do be aware of the destructive cults that try to gain control or cults that distinguish themselves from a normal social or religious group. Four techniques to watch for are: Behavior control, thought control, emotional control, and/or information control. These techniques can be used together to make a total web, which can manipulate even the strongest minded people. In fact, it is the strongest minded individuals who make the most involved and enthusiastic cult members. People under this mind control are not aware of it.

Elementals-Look after the earth and are also referred to as nature angels. Unlike heavenly angels, they do have egos.

ESP-Extrasensory perception is a collective term for various mental abilities. The ability of human beings to perceive things beyond the scope of known bodily senses; some types include telepathy, clairvoyance, or precognition.

Metaphysical-A philosophy that deals with first principles and seeks to explain nature and reality; goes beyond mere physical senses.

Monotheism-A belief in one God: Judaism, Christianity, and Islamic faiths.

Mystic-One who penetrates the material world of sensations. They function on high senses. They take all five senses (sight, sound, smell, taste, and touch) to the highest degree.

OM-Not necessarily a word, but a sound or vibration; said to be the sound the universe made in creation. Sounds like the word home without the h. Used as a mantra to calm and quiet; can be used in meditation.

Oracle Cards-Cards used to provide an insight for those seeking answers to inner questions. Have you ever wished that you could ask a spirit, an angel, or even your own pet a question and receive the answers, but know your own ears won't hear it? An answer is possible through these cards. Different types of cards are available; they should be chosen according to your own specific attraction to them.

Physic-Is beyond natural or of the physical process. Physic is sensitive to forces beyond the physical world. In Biblical times, the word spirit was used for physic. Ex. "He was in spirit."

Polytheistic-Many Gods—Believe God is everywhere, including within nature. These paths work with angels, goddesses, elementals (another name for nature angels), and other deities.

Psychiatrist-A medical doctor (MD) who may also perform psychotherapy (study of the mind). Can also prescribe medications and perform medical procedures.

Psychologist-May hold a PhD (doctoral-level degree), but is not a medical doctor. Can assist patient through counseling and psychotherapy.

Psychotherapy-Generally a longer term treatment which focuses on gaining insight into chronic physical and emotional problems; requires more skill than mere counseling. Psychotherapy is conducted by professionals trained to practice, such as a psychiatrists, social workers, trained counselor, or psychologists.

Reflexology-Reflexology, or zone therapy, is an alternative medicine involving the physical act of applying pressure to the feet, hands, or ears. These areas correspond to other areas of the body, and by working on these, you can improve health.

Spirit/Soul-Does not refer to any religion or belief. It radiates from deep within us outward. It is the essence of your being that lives forever. The soul is the essence that inhabits physical form, while the spirit is the part that connects to the perceived "Divine" source.

Ying/Yang-Male/female. Positive/negative. Light/dark.

Resources

I would like to share the following resources. I am not paid to endorse them, and I only share what has encouraged and continues to inspire me. When we focus on our strengths, we become strong. When we focus on weaknesses, we stay weak. May these resources offer you support to stay strong on those days you need a companion's hand or a loved one's hug.

Pep Talks and Encouraging Reads:
Daily Insights - mydailyinsights.com
Dale Carnegie - book sources
Dyer, Dr. Wayne - drwaynedyer.com
Elko, Dr. Kevin - drelko.com
Hayes, Louise - Hayhouse.com
Peale, Dr. Norman Vincent - book sources
Rodgers, Vimala-Your Handwriting Can Change
    Your Life - iihs.com
Rupp, Joyce - joycerupp.com
Sounds True - Soundstrue.com
Stephen C. Paul - circledancer.com
Virtue, Doreen - AngelTherapy.com

Inspiring/Healing Music:
Gratitude Joy - realmusic.com
Inner Worlds Music - Merlin's Angel Symphony and
    Angel Helpers - innerworldsmusic.com
Jonathan Goldman - healingsounds.com
Marina Raye-Circle of Compassion - marinaray.com
Siddhayoga music - bookstore.siddhayoga.org

Energy Medicine:
Barbara Brennan - barbarabrennan.com
Donna Eden - innersource.com (&)
    learnenergymedicine.com
International Institute of Reflexology –
    reflexology-usa.net

Reflexology Science Institute - reflexologyscience.com
How to do reflexology–how-to-do-reflexology.com
Web page with charts Stacy Simone - littleepiphany.com/massage/foot chart
Self-Healing - taoofwellness.com (Gi Gong and other energy techniques)

Health Related:
(As of the date of publication, these websites/phone numbers are current.)
Braga Organics. The site carries organic nuts, seeds, and jams. - buyorganicnuts.com
H.Acres. Health food and supplements. hacres.com
Hippocrates Health Institute. Supplements and a health magazine. - hippocratesinst.org
Hormone information and test kits - Dr. John R. Lee & Virginia Hopkins - johnleemd.com
Jaffe Bros. Untreated fruits, nuts, seeds, dehydrated vegetables, and other organic items. organicfruitsandnuts.com

Supplements:
Hippocrates Institute 1-877-582-5850 hippocratesinst.org
Pure Encapsulations 1-800-753-2277 pureencapsulations.com
Pure Synergy 1-800-723-0277 TheSynergyCompany.com
Thorne Research-Thorne.com

Hormone testing kits and hormones:
Moundsville Pharmacy-Bio-identical hormones and

testing kits; will ship anywhere. moundsvillepharmacy.com

Women's International Health. Bio-identical hormones; will ship anywhere. womensinternational.com

ZRT. Hormones, cortisol, vitamin D, iodine, cardio metabolic profiles and blood spot test kits. zrtlab.com

Renee Salvatori

> *"A thank-you comes from the joyful pulse of the heart."*
> —Renee Salvatori

Acknowledgements

Thank you to my husband for your unending support. You took over domestic duties so I could travel to the library on Saturdays to write in silence. You overlooked my far-off stare and forgave me for having a relationship with my writings instead of with you. You have taken my beginning writings and patiently edited them. Thank you!

Also, I thank my children for your patience as I worked on this project. I owe you big thanks for your assistance with the computer. You were my rescue team when I couldn't convince it to do something it was not built to do. Thank you to my daughter for helping me with the charts and typesetting. I do not need to be convinced that my children are smarter than I am.

Thank you to my mother for all those words that still have me searching. Thank you to my sisters for their encouragement. You all have made me into a permanent seeker.

Thank you to my family and non-blood family, friends, neighbors, teachers, and strangers I have learned from. Earth angels are abundant, and I have learned from you all.

Thank you to my editors and artistic team at Written Dreams: Brittiany Koren, Susan Pawlicki, Eddie Vincent, and Logan Stefonek. You are all wonderful people.

Also, thank you, celestial heavens, for helping me. I continue to look up for your guidance and support.

With My Love,
—Renee

About the Authors

Renee Salvatori lives in West Virginia with her husband and four children, where she home schools one son. She continues to learn at the feet of her children; they are her best teachers. She has a passion for writing, journaling, and reading. It was this passion for writing that persuaded her to share her experiences with others.

Before staying home to raise her children, she worked in the health field. She has always been eager to understand ways of healing the body physically, mentally, and emotionally. She has always tried many new ways for healing and continues to apply what works for her. She is nicknamed the perpetual seeker. She feels that life is too short not to seek all you can.

She is passionate about personal growth and healing of all kinds. Finding ways to improve her life, the lives of those she loves, and those she doesn't even know yet. She feels that life is not always pretty, but it can offer you a wonderful learning opportunity. She takes those opportunities of past and shares them from her heart.

For more information, please visit Renee's website at www.reneesalvatori.com.

Mary Roberts is a free spirit and very open-minded. A reformed alcoholic, she began her renewal on life at age twenty-four and has been much happier ever since. She is currently working on a cook book and other professional pursuits. She lives in Colorado with her husband, singer/songwriter/composer and Colorado Music Hall of Famer Rick Roberts.

www.ingramcontent.com/pod-product-compliance
Lightning Source LLC
Chambersburg PA
CBHW021125300426
44113CB00006B/296